POLICE SUICIDE

POLICE SUICIDE

Tactics for Prevention

Edited by

DELL P. HACKETT

President, Law Enforcement Wellness Association

and

JOHN M. VIOLANTI, Ph.D.

Department of Criminal Justice
Rochester Institute of Technology
Rochester, New York
Department of Social and Preventative Medicine
School of Medical and Biomedical Sciences
State University of New York at Buffalo
Buffalo, New York

With a Foreword by
James T. Reese, Ph.D.
FBI, Retired
Lake Ridge, Virginia

CHARLES C THOMAS • PUBLISHER, LTD.
Springfield • Illinois • U.S.A.

Published and Distributed Throughout the World by

CHARLES C THOMAS • PUBLISHER, LTD.
2600 South First Street
Springfield, Illinois 62704

ISBN 0-398-07334-1 (hard)
ISBN 0-398-07335-X (paper)

Library of Congress Catalog Card Number: 2002069574

With THOMAS BOOKS *careful attention is given to all details of manufacturing
and design. It is the Publisher's desire to present books that are satisfactory as to their
physical qualities and artistic possibilities and appropriate for their particular use.*
THOMAS BOOKS *will be true to those laws of quality that assure a good name
and good will.*

Printed in the United States of America
RR-R-3

Library of Congress Cataloging-in-Publication Data

Police suicide : tactics for prevention and intervention/ edited by Dell P. Hackett
and John M. Violanti
    p. cm.
  Includes bibliographical references and index
  ISBN 0-398-07334-1 –– ISBN 0-398-07335-X (pbk)
  1. Police––Suicidal behavior––United States. 2. Police––Job stress––United States 3.
Suicide––Prevention. I. Hackett, Dell P. II. Violanti, John M.

HV7936.S77 P65 2002
362.2'8'0883632––dc21   2002069574

CONTRIBUTORS

Daniel W. Clark, Ph.D.

Dr. Clark presently serves as a clinical psychologist with the Washington State Patrol, Olympia, Washington. He has worked with individual, marital, and family evaluation and treatment of employees and family members; consulted with department supervisors and managers regarding employee situations, management dilemmas, suspect profile development, and disaster situations; conducted pre-employment psychological evaluations of trooper cadets; conducted psychological evaluations for specialty positions; directed the Peer Support and Critical Incident Teams; provided instruction in stress management, critical incident stress, time management, death notification, communication, suicide intervention, and related topics. He has also recently conducted individual and group evaluation and treatment of the 20,000 1st Armored Division soldiers deployed to Operations Desert Shield/Storm; instruction of soldiers and commanders on battle fatigue prevention and treatment; organizational and individual consultation to unit commanders and leaders; supervision of mental health counselors. Dr. Clark has many presentations and publications in the areas of stress, posttraumatic stress disorder, and emergency work trauma.

Dickson Diamond, M.D.

Dr. Diamond is presently the Chief Psychiatrist for the FBI and the Chief Medical Officer for National Domestic Preparedness, Washington, DC. He has previously been employed by the Central Intelligence Agency, Washington, DC, as a Psychiatric Medical Officer (1994–1998). Dr. Diamond is a past chair of Federal Law

Enforcement Suicide Prevention Working Group Task Force Member—Department of Justice, Office for Victims of Crime, and the American College of Forensic Examiners Board of Law Enforcement Experts. He has an academic appointment as Clinical Professor of Psychiatry, George Washington School of Medicine. His past writings include contributions to the *On-Scene Commander's Guide for Responding to Biological/Chemical Threats*.

Claudia L. Greene, M.D.

Dr. Greene is a law enforcement physician board certified in anatomic pathology and board eligible in psychiatry. She has 30 years street experience studying physical and psychic violence, aggression, and trauma. She has studied physical and psychic patterns of injury not only in those involved in violent interactions. She has focused not only on physical and psychic injury, but also on human resiliency and the core human issues of trust/mistrust, normal and abnormal development of the self, and how all of these parameters come together in violence, aggression, and other crimes. She is currently chronicling her knowledge in a comprehensive book for law enforcement, the fire service, and emergency medical services titled *Reading the Street*. Dr. Greene received her medical degree from the University of Texas Southwestern Medical School in Dallas, did an internship in general surgery at Baylor University Medical Center in Dallas, a residency in anatomic pathology at Parkland and Baylor hospitals in Dallas, and a cytopathology fellowship at Baylor in Dallas. She was named a member of Psychological Services of the Dallas Police Department and has been the psychiatric consultant for the Dallas District of the Federal Bureau of Investigation for more than ten years. She has been active in critical incident stress debriefing (beginning with the Waco Branch Davidian affair and continuing with other high profile situations) and crisis negotiation and other law enforcement training. She is currently the director of *CopSolutions* , a nationally based teaching team focusing on state-of-the-art technical training for law enforcement officers. Dr. Greene has special expertise and interest in preventive mental health for police officers.

Dell P. Hackett

Dell P. Hackett is a recently retired police lieutenant from the Lane County Sheriff's Office, Eugene, Oregon, and president of the Law Enforcement Wellness Association (LEWA). LEWA has been instrumental in conducting training seminars throughout the country in police peer support, stress, and police suicide. On his promotion to lieutenant in 1991, Mr. Hackett was assigned as the assistant division commander of the 62-member Police Services Division. Duties included division middle management responsibility and supplying direct supervision to eight first-line supervisors (sergeants). Other areas of responsibility included management of the law enforcement function for two contract cities within Lane county. Additional duties included team leader and team commander within the department's special weapons and tactics unit (SWAT). Mr. Hackett belongs to numerous professional associations, including the American Academy of Experts on Traumatic Stress and the American College of Forensic Examiners where he holds a Diplomate status. He is also a graduate of the FBI National Academy.

Robert Loo, Ph.D.

Dr. Robert Loo is currently Professor of Human Resource Management and Organizational Studies in the Faculty of Management at the University of Lethbridge, Alberta, Canada. He started his professional career as an infantry officer in the Canadian army in the 1960s with NATO and UN service. He has changed careers several times since then, with management positions in the high-tech industry and the federal government before joining the University of Lethbridge in 1989. Dr. Loo has a long-standing interest in occupational stress but he first addressed police suicide when he joined the Royal Canadian Mounted Police Headquarters in 1982 as their first Chief Psychologist. Dr. Loo has published extensively in the occupational stress field and continues to have a special concern for those who serve and protect—police officers.

Paul Quinnett, Ph.D.

Dr. Quinnett is clinical psychologist with more than 30 years experience in both public and private practice. He is the Chief Psychologist for Spokane Mental Health's APA-approved internship in psychology and serves as Clinical Assistant Professor in the Department of Psychiatry and Behavioral Science at the University of Washington School of Medicine. A Washington State University graduate, he also serves as Clinical Director of Greentree Behavioral Health at Holy Family Hospital and President and CEO of the QPR Institute, a national training and research organization devoted to the prevention of suicide. Among other professional titles, he is the author of *Suicide: The Forever Decision* and *Counseling Suicidal People: A Therapy of Hope*. An avid fisherman and award-winning outdoor writer, he is also the author of *Pavlov's Trout, Darwin's Bass* and *Fishing Lessons*, the first books published on psychology and philosophy of life and fishing in 300 years.

James T. Reese, Ph.D.

Dr. Reese is the CEO of James T. Reese and Associates, a Virginia-based international behavioral sciences and management-consulting firm. An author, lecturer, and consultant, Dr. Reese is board certified as an Expert in Stress Management, Emergency Crisis Response, and Acute Traumatic Stress Management. He is a Fellow of the American Academy of Experts in Traumatic Stress and is a Diplomate in Police and Criminal Psychology. He served as a platoon leader in Vietnam, and after 25 years as an FBI Agent, he retired as the Assistant Unit Chief of the Behavioral Science Unit. He lectured at the FBI Academy for 18 years on stress, leadership, profiling, and more. Dr. Reese helped to establish the psychological services program, the employee assistance program, and the stress management program at the FBI. He was one of the founders of the National Center for the Analysis of Violent Crime. He published seven books while in the FBI. Dr. Reese has presented to representatives of more than 300 Fortune 500 companies. www.jamestreese.com

Teresa Tidwell-Tate

Ms. Tate is a widow of a police officer who committed suicide in 1989 and is an advocate for survivors of law enforcement suicide. She has established a network for survivors of law enforcement suicide through the creation of a newsletter and offers assistance to law enforcement agencies when a suicide has occurred. She is also credited for the development and implementation of the Survivor of Suicide support group, in Lee County, Florida. While employed with the Bureau of Alcohol, Tobacco and Firearms (ATF), Ms. Tate was a member of ATF's peer support team and attended several critical incident/peer support training seminars. Over the years, Ms. Tate has been requested to assist law enforcement families from various agencies affected by suicide and non-suicidal deaths, as well as special agents involved in shooting incidents. Ms. Tate provided guidance and policy recommendations in developing ATF's Spousal Support Program. Ms. Tate has written articles on law enforcement suicide for various magazines and newsletters for law enforcement organizations. Ms. Tate has been a guest on several radio talk shows, including "America Under Siege" which is sponsored by the National Law Enforcement Officers Memorial. In February 1997, Ms. Tate was a speaker at a suicide conference for police officers that was sponsored by the Fraternal Order of Police. In September 1999, Ms. Tate presented a paper titled, "Police Suicides: Assessing the Needs of the Survivors" at the FBI Academy. This paper was presented during the Suicide and Law Enforcement Symposium. In November 1999, Ms. Tate was a speaker at the first National Survivors for Suicide Prevention Day which was hosted by the American Foundation for Suicide Prevention. Ms. Tate is listed as a resource in several books, including *I Love A Cop*, by Dr. Ellen Kirschman and *Copshock* by Allen Kates. In April 1998, Ms. Tate designed a banner in which 21 law enforcement agencies participated in memorializing those officers who died by their own hand. This banner is displayed annually during a remembrance ceremony at the U.S. Capitol.

John M. Violanti, Ph.D.

John M. Violanti, Ph.D., is an Associate Clinical Professor at the

State University of New York at Buffalo School of Medicine, Department of Social and Preventive Medicine, and Associate Professor at the Rochester Institute of Technology (RIT) Rochester, New York, in Criminal Justice. Professor Violanti is a retired 23-year veteran of the New York State Police, serving as a trooper and an investigator with the Bureau of Criminal Investigation. During the last few years of his police career, Dr. Violanti helped to establish and coordinate the first psychological and employee assistance program for the State Police. Dr. Violanti's research interests include psychological stress, trauma stress, and police suicide.

Vickie M. Watson, M.S., N.C.A.C.

Ms. Watson is the National Training Director for the QPR Institute and has been involved with the QPR program since its inception. She has more than 20 years of clinical experience and has worked in many facets of mental health and chemical dependency treatment as a therapist, clinical supervisor, program manager and presenter of national training activities. In addition to her extensive experience in suicide prevention, risk assessment, and risk management, she is also active in providing postvention services and working with survivors of grief and trauma. She resides in Spokane, Washington.

Elizabeth K. White, Ph.D.

Dr. White is a clinical psychologist presently with the Los Angeles Sheriff's Department Employee Support Services Bureau . Her work includes clinical tasks such as conducting family, individual, and couples therapy with department members and their dependents on both work-related and non-work-related issues. She also coordinates treatment with outside clinicians as needed and provides group counseling on specific topics such as earthquakes and parenting. Dr. White has significant training responsibilities across several mediums. Direct training obligations include academy classes and special unit classes: Stress Management–Field Personnel, Stress Management–Custody Personnel, Law Enforcement Suicide Prevention/Intervention for Supervisors, Critical Incident Stress

Management, Dealing with a Critical Incident for Line Staff, Orientation Program for Law Enforcement Spouses, Introduction to Employee Support Services, Smoking Cessation, Coping With Change, etc. She was responsible for the Peer Support Three Day Training Course and the four Quarterly Update trainings conducted each year on a variety of topics such as Anger Management, Parent/Child Problems, Supervisor/Subordinate Problems, Recovering from an Affair, and Relationship Problems. Training requirements involved direct training, as well as securing outside instructors on specialty topics. She is also responsible for training the Officer Involved Shooter Team and for the Critical Incident Stress Management Team. Dr. White has numerous publications and presentations in the area of police psychology.

This book is dedicated to the police officers, firefighters, rescue workers, and emergency personnel, who, without regard for their own safety, faced the brutal terrorist attack on New York City and Washington, DC, on September 11, 2001.

FOREWORD

The mysteries of our minds continue to be hidden in dark and elusive theories, postulates, axioms, and philosophies. None of these, however, serves all purposes. Scientists and psychologists have forever wondered how one person's mind can create a philosopher whereas another mind creates a concert pianist. Why does one person become a criminal and another invests his or her life in the enforcement of laws? Why would one individual never consider taking the life of another, yet the same person would consider taking their own life? Obviously, there remains a dark side of the mind. A side that evades the light of understanding.

I have had the pleasure of knowing the editors of this book for years, both personally and professionally. During that time, it has continuously been the focus in their farseeing eyes to explore, and hopefully shed light on, the issues surrounding police suicides.

Scientists have long said that income, occupation, and education are the most important predictors of people's health and how long they will live. But they have no way of telling which one has had the greatest impact or whether any may be the cause of one's decision to end life. It is my opinion that education leads the field as the emerging and most critical predictor of longevity and health. It is what we do not know that can hurt us. This should come as good news to those of us who are trying to ward off the potential onslaught of suicides. The news is grim for those who choose not to look to education as a solution. They will find themselves on the wrong side of the gap that exists between myth and reality.

If any other portion of the American population had a pronounced increase in their mortality rate because of suicide, it would be considered unacceptable, and millions of dollars would be designated for research. Not so for the lonely police officer on the beat. It is not considered a national disaster by most. It is, however, for those of us who have dedicated our lives to serve and protect others.

The range of information in this book is broad and offers strategies and tactics that may help to prevent suicides. The book contains far more than that which would usually come to mind concerning the subject of self-destructive behavior. The focus of the book concerns diverse and very important areas such as the police culture, the supervisor's role in intervention, departmental denial of the problem, getting officers to seek help, family issues, and survivor issues. All are intended to get the reader closer to being able to identify officers who may be in harms way, offer solutions to those who seek help, and hopefully prevent police suicides. This book is interesting, useful, and understandable.

No other time in police history has offered such promise. Only recently has the identification of police stress and the subsequent counterproductive behaviors been exposed and accepted within the culture. However, there are still pockets of departmental and administrative resistance. We have learned that the police occupation is different from all others and that it is all right to be different. It is the hope that information in this book will prevent future suicides and even reverse the thinking that leads to such life-ending decisions.

This new understanding may also provide a potential remedy for some of law enforcement's greatest ills—alcohol abuse, family abuse, and the subsequent consequences. I believe that this book will be interesting and useful to those who would read it with the intention of understanding this dilemma faced by law enforcement and a continued desire to search for possible solutions.

Read this book. Early education is required if we are to stem the tide of suicides in law enforcement. This book is a "must read" for law enforcement officers, probation and parole officers, supervisors, mental health professionals, educators, criminal justice students, and professors. Virtually every one of us must get involved, so that our society can continue to be protected by the dedicated law enforcement officers that walk our streets. This book is complete and well researched. It is a cooperative effort, not a competitive one; a journey of discovery and hope.

James T. Reese, Ph.D., FBI Retired
Fellow, American Academy of Experts in Traumatic Stress
Diplomate, Society of Police and Criminal Psychology
James T. Reese and Associates, Lake Ridge, VA
www.jamestreese.com

PREFACE

Suicide within the ranks of law enforcement is not a new problem. It is expected by the public that law enforcement officers deal with death, misery, and the very worst of the human condition. As law enforcement administrators, we attempt to provide our personnel with the very best physical tools possible. The best radios, weapons, vehicles, and bullet-resistant vests; however, we haven't done an adequate job of offering the training and awareness that can "bullet proof" the mind. It is no secret that depression, substance abuse, domestic abuse, and suicide can be the silent partners of law enforcement.

This book was written by several skilled and caring professionals. It is hoped that the information contained within can give law enforcement officers, administrators, and mental health professionals additional information and skills in dealing with law enforcement officers in crisis. The experts agree that 80 percent–90 percent of those individuals completing suicide often communicate their suicidal intent to someone. To the untrained, these usually subtle communications are often ignored. On the flip side, a successful intervention, applied by those trained in suicide prevention/intervention skills, has been proven to save lives. Law enforcement peers, supervisors, and administrators are in an ideal position to monitor the psychological wellness of their department members. The key words here are training and awareness. Training and awareness equal the confidence to recognize the suicidal danger signs and ask the right questions, at the right time. In simple terms, ask a question, save a life.

I firmly believe we are in the midst of a positive culture change regarding psychological wellness in law enforcement. In most progressive and professional law enforcement agencies, it is no longer considered a sign of weakness to seek psychological counseling. There are still pockets of resistance to this issue, but in general we are getting better. Law enforcement officers who avail themselves of psychological assistance are approaching the issue from a position of strength, not weakness.

I would like to personally thank my partner in this endeavor, Dr. John Violanti. There is no one who has contributed more to the study and research of police suicide than John Violanti. John's ongoing research, his willingness to share his findings, and his true compassion for law enforcement officers have made a positive difference in the manner in which we are dealing with the extremely complex issues of law enforcement suicide.

Lt. (Ret.) Dell P. Hackett
28-Year Police Veteran

AUTHOR'S NOTE

Dell P. Hackett and I compiled this book to bring together some of the knowledge of experts in the field of suicide and suicide prevention. Our goal was to make this knowledge accessible to those who work in policing, as well as academicians. We hope that this information will be just one of many resources to lead toward effective prevention of the tragedy of police suicide.

J.M.V.

CONTENTS

POLICE SUICIDE

Chapter 1

POLICE SUICIDE: TACTICS FOR PREVENTION

JOHN M. VIOLANTI

There has been increased interest in prevention of suicide among police officers. Such interest is a result of new evidence that the police have a greater risk of suicide than other professions and the general population.

We are, however, faced with many challenges in prevention efforts. One challenge is that we do not yet know the scope of the problem. Police suicide may actually be much higher than we presently estimate. Second is the consuming denial by police departments that suicide is a problem. Suicide prevention is often not included in training programs, and no one wants to admit that suicide may exist in high proportions within their own profession. Third is our lack of sufficient information as to why police suicide occurs. We have some information on this, but much more in-depth research is needed to help clarify issues of stress, posttraumatic stress disorder, alcohol use, depression, and relationship problems among police.

This book first gives a brief overview of possible strategies and tactics that may help to prevent police suicide. In Chapter 2, Hackett first discusses the important role of the police supervisors in suicide prevention, commenting that supervisors are in an excellent position to monitor and help subordinates get help. Also discussed are peer support programs as sources of support and as "safe places" for officers to help resolve their problems. Last, Hackett briefly overviews a suicide prevention program that involves supervisory training, suicide awareness, and methods of communicating with possible suicidal officers.

In Chapter 3, Clark and White discuss the important and often complex relationship between mental health clinicians, police officers, and getting help. Clark and White explore the reason for mistrust of the mental health system by officers. Last, they explore in detail issues as to why it is so difficult for law enforcement officers to seek help and what family, partners, supervisors, and friends can do to help.

Quinnet and Watson discuss their method of "QPR" (question-persuade-refer) for suicide prevention and its application to law enforcement in Chapter 4. QPR has particular application to law enforcement environments, both within a department and through employee assistance programs (EAPs). The nature of close-knit associations and the necessity of teamwork make the training of officers in QPR a necessity. It is often co-workers on the force who may be in the most likely position to see warning signs of risk that could lead to a life-saving intervention. Similarly, spouses and family members may pick up on different clues. More opportunities for early intervention exist when members of a socially integrated organization (including families) are trained to recognize a potential suicide crisis in progress and are trained in what steps to take to interrupt the suicidal journey.

In Chapter 5, Diamond provides a psychiatrist's viewpoint of suicide in policing. Central to Dr. Diamond's idea is that depression plays a major part in police suicide and that many factors previously mentioned as precedents to suicide actually are precedents to depression. He encourages police managers and departments to become familiar with depression, because it affects such a high percentage of officers, especially when this depression is associated with a significant risk for suicide. The symptoms of clinical depression include a decrease in energy or increased fatigue and a loss of the ability to partake in enjoyable activities. A good manager will recognize these symptoms, they are the telltale clues that an officer has depression. A feeling of sadness, worry, and desperation tend to dominate one's thoughts. Officers with clinical depression must expend excess amounts of energy during work hours just to fight off these debilitating symptoms of depression and maintain a relatively competent level of functioning. Officers who have worked in particularly stressful environments or who have encountered significant traumatic situations on the job will experience an even greater impact.

Violanti discusses the impact of police culture on suicide in Chapter 6. Entry into law enforcement involves a process of abrupt change from citizen to police officer. The rookie officer's adaptation of a new work role occurs interactively at individual and social levels. The process of change from civilian to police officer is very strong in basic police training and continues to dominate officer's lives throughout their career. Thus, as a consequence, officers may deal with most life situations, good or bad, from the standpoint of their police role. This raises the question of the impact of the police role on life relationships that may precipitate psychological stress–personal, police peer, and societal relationships. Violanti discusses the process of police cultural influence on the mental health and life circumstances of police officers that may increase the potential for suicide.

In Chapter 7 , Greene provides a psychiatric orientation on police officers who cannot trust others to help them. She emphasizes how trust may have an impact on the officer's decision to seek help for difficult life and work problems. Others may notice the non-trusting officer pulling away in interpersonal interactions and begin to question the officers actions. They express their concern and may ask him repeatedly what is wrong. The more they want to help, the less trusting the officer becomes. A vicious circle begins. The harder his loved ones and colleagues knock at the door and ask to be let in, the more nails the officer puts in the door. The officer gradually builds a silent barrier between himself and the ones concerned about him and his lack of trust. The people trying to help the officer describe him as interpersonal; the shield has "gone up." In many cases, it is impenetrable, even by mental health professionals.

In Chapter 8, Loo outlines tactics for dealing with suicide after it occurs in a police agency. His discussion centers on "postvention" and procedures that will deal with present and possible future suicides. Postvention is seen as a natural extension to the established suicide prevention field, partly because there will always be some base level of suicide, even when highly effective suicide prevention programs exist, and partly because the survivors of a suicide can be viewed as victims of posttraumatic stress and, therefore, in need of assistance in dealing with their grief reaction.

Chapter 9 concerns the needs of police suicide survivors, especially the officers' family. Theresa Tate, founder of Survivors of Law Enforcement Suicide (SOLES), discusses how the police agency can better help survivors of suicide. The actions and reactions of the police chief down to the patrol officer will forever be remembered by a survivor. The trauma that survivors experience may vary from visual effects, to improper notification, to department speculation, to lack of compassion toward survivors. The survivor, as well as the police department, will embark on a painful journey for years to come.

The increased risk of police suicide is not a myth or insignificant problem, it is an indication of the intolerable strain placed on the police officer's work and life roles. Dell Hackett and I hope that this book will add to previous writings and provide clearer direction for dealing with suicide in the ranks of policing. Certainly, this edition does not finish the task. It may only serve as a first-step guide to mental health clinicians, police supervisors, friends, and family to stop the tragic death of loved ones and our national heroes.

Chapter 2

SUICIDE AND THE POLICE

DELL P. HACKETT

INTRODUCTION

In an occupation wrought with the potential of personal assault, murder, death investigation, and exposure to many other tragedies, is there an increased risk of suicide within the ranks of the nation's police? The evidence is fairly conclusive regarding this question. Field and Jones (1999) in a definitive article in *USA Today* quoted the following statistics obtained from several of the nation's larger law enforcement agencies:

1. *New York City PD, 1985–1998:*–Suicides = 87; line of duty deaths =36;
   department size = 40,000; compared with national suicide rate: + 29.1 percent
2. *Chicago PD, 1990–1998:*–Suicides = 22; line of duty deaths = 12;
   department size = 13,500; compared with national suicide rate: + 50.9 percent
3. *FBI, 1993-1998:*–Suicides = 18; line of duty deaths = 4;
   department size = 11,500; compared with national suicide rate: +116.6 percent
4. *Los Angeles PD 1990–1998*: Suicides = 20; line of duty deaths = 11;
   department size = 9,668; compared with national suicide rate: +72.5 percent
5. *San Diego PD, 1992-1998*: Suicides = 5; line of duty deaths = 0;

department size = 2,000; compared with national suicide rate: + 197.5 percent

It seems obvious that there is an increased risk for suicide within the law enforcement profession. Indeed, more law enforcement officers take their own lives each year than are killed by felons or die in other duty-related accidents (Turvey, 1997). By the very nature of the law enforcement profession, stresses that can lead to suicidal thinking are many. In a survey of 500 law enforcement officers done by The National P.O.L.I.C.E. Suicide Foundation, Inc. (1998), 98 percent of the officers said they would consider suicide and cited the following reasons:

- Death of a child or spouse
- Loss of a child or spouse through divorce
- Terminal illness
- Responsibility for co-workers death
- Killed someone out of anger
- Indictment
- Feeling alone
- Sexual accusations
- Loss of job because of conviction of a crime
- Being locked up

SUICIDE PREVENTION STRATEGIES

Traditionally, police officers view themselves as rugged, stand-alone individuals. Law enforcement officers routinely deal with the problems of others yet often deny or attempt to bury their own. Within the police culture, officers who are experiencing psychological problems can be viewed as weak and sometimes a "bad fit" for the profession. This attitude has been responsible for officers remaining silent and not seeking the psychological assistance they may need. It is often not until the officers individual situation reaches crisis proportion, such as in a suicide, that a department will acknowledge there may have been a problem.

Although personal intervention is certainly necessary in preventing suicide, police departmental changes and training can effectively add to any prevention protocol. The following strategies may help to prevent officers from reaching that point in their lives when they think of committing suicide.

The Role of the Police Supervisor in Suicide Prevention

The law enforcement first-line supervisor, when properly trained, is in an excellent position to monitor his or her subordinates for signs of distress that could lead to a suicide. Generally, the supervisor is in daily contact with subordinates and can spot-check the overall emotional wellness of line officers on a regular basis. These spot-checks can be done during briefing sessions, evaluation periods, meal breaks, or any impromptu meeting that may occur during the work shift. Kates (1999) discusses critical incident stress exposure and the correlation of the exposure to the onset of severe post traumatic stress disorder. The signs and symptoms of an individual in crisis as a result of critical incident stress can mirror the warning signs of suicide. The supervisor is in a position to ensure proper critical incident debriefing procedures, and follow-up care is given to those employees potentially affected by a traumatic event. The ability and skill to recognize suicidal symptoms and behavior in subordinates comes through structured training, caring, and compassion. Furthermore, good supervisors realize the personnel that make up a law enforcement agency are the most important and valued resources. This chapter will discuss the law enforcement agencies' role and responsibility in suicide prevention and intervention training. First-line supervisors can have a dramatic impact on the prevention of suicide within their agencies. With training in suicide prevention and intervention tactics, the law enforcement supervisor could literally save the lives of those he or she leads.

Supervisors need to closely observe and learn the personality characteristics of those they are assigned to lead. One-on-one meetings should be conducted between the supervisor and his or her subordinates on a regular basis. This is an excellent means by which clues of possible depression, anxiety , or a host of other psychological maladies can be noted and a possible intervention started. It is highly recommended that departments incorporate supervisory training narrowly and specifically related to the warning signs of those officers that may be considering suicide. Although the reasons for suicide are many and often complex, the supervisor is in an excellent position to identify and lead those employees in crisis to treatment. The warning signs exhibited by officers contemplating suicide are often easily observable to the trained eye.

Slovenko (Violanti, 1996) estimates that 80 percent of suicide victims give off clues regarding their intentions to kill themselves. Supervisors should attend structured training in the verbal, behavioral, coded, and situational clues of those contemplating suicide. Not only is it important for supervisors to recognize suicidal behavior, they should also know the intervention steps necessary for those in need of treatment. All law enforcement agencies should have a mental health professional identified and trained in dealing with law enforcement psychological trauma. These same mental health professionals should have training specific to the treatment of law enforcement officers and be familiar with the increased risk of suicide within the law enforcement profession.

Peer Support Programs in Law Enforcement

The prevention of suicide requires a strong support system. To the police officer, no one is better qualified to understand "the job" more than another police officer. Peer support programs seem to work well for suicide intervention.

Peer support within law enforcement agencies is hardly a new concept. Law enforcement officers have always confided in their peers when the going gets tough. Each agency seems to have those individuals that are natural, often informal, leaders to which others are drawn during difficult times. These trusted co-workers are usually natural listeners and very adept at communication skills. Most of all they are trusted, approachable, and compassionate. In a nutshell, they have that ability to help others through difficult times and get them back on track.

Peer support and counseling can most accurately be described as a process whereby officers who feel a need to communicate their feelings about the job, their home life, or a combination of the two may do so with other officers that are trained to assist. In structured law enforcement peer support programs, peer counselors are formally trained by mental health professionals in topical areas such as counseling skills, crisis theory and intervention, early warning signs of prolonged or acute stress, suicide assessment, alcohol and substance abuse, and matters of confidentiality. Overall, the peer counselors' mission is to provide a confidential outlet and then decide whether further referral to a mental health professional is necessary. Peer support personnel should never attempt to conduct clinical therapy. Only certified professionals who are trained in treating law enforcement officers can provide therapy and determine the proper course of treatment for an officer in need of professional assistance.

The selection of peer support personnel is critical to the success of the program. Much like other specialty units within an agency (SWAT, Negotiation Teams, Bomb Squads, etc.), the success or failure of the unit depends on the selection of only the best and most qualified for the assignment. Those selected must be trusted and held in high esteem by their co-workers. They must be sensitive to racial diversity and multicultural issues within their agencies. In determining the number of peer support personnel to train, the size of the department is the obvious consideration. An entire article can be written on the selection of peer support personnel. Suffice it to say that only the most respected and trusted volunteers should be considered. Anything less can doom a program to failure.

The Impact of Suicide on the Department

It is important for leaders to understand that the entire agency is emotionally and negatively impacted when a suicide occurs within its ranks. The suicide of a co-worker is listed as one of the top eight critical incidents within the emergency services profession (Mitchell, 1990). Most law enforcement agencies, or specific work units within larger agencies, bear significant resemblance to close-knit families. Law enforcement officers often view each other as teammates, comrades, and members of a proud and demanding profession. By the very nature of law enforcement work, police officers must count on each other in dangerous, sometimes life-threatening, situations.

The suicide of a department member can send the agency or a specific work unit into an emotional tailspin that can take months, if not years, in which to recover. Law enforcement suicides, much like line of duty deaths, can severely and dramatically impact the emotional well-being of fellow officers and other co-workers. Ralph

Slovenko (Violanti, 1996) states *"Police Suicides can devastate the morale of entire agencies and leave individual officers with intense feelings of guilt, remorse, and disillusionment; many feel they should have done something to prevent the suicide"* (p. ix).

Still, today, many departmental leaders still insist that suicide will never occur in their department, or that "only one or two have occurred here in the past twenty years." Denial seems to be the order of the day. Many refuse to acknowledge law enforcement suicide as an occupational problem that requires formal training (Turvey, 1997). Baker (1996), in a very influential article on police suicide prevention states, ". . . the affected officers often resist seeking help for fear of losing their jobs, being demoted, or having their personal problems exposed for public ridicule. These common systemic reactions must be overcome before any successful intervention can take place. Many officers feel that referral to a mental health professional would mean the loss of their jobs. Police supervisors have a similar value system, and because of this belief, they often fail to take the appropriate action."

A POLICE SUICIDE PREVENTION MODEL

The training recommended for police first-line supervisors should be conducted by a mental health professional with the assistance of a respected, trained, police officer. Law enforcement officers traditionally hold a general distrust for many mental health professionals Finding a trusted mental health professional in conjunction with a trusted peer will greatly enhance the manner in which the training is received. The training should be broken down into segments.

- The statistics around police suicide. Compare and contrast law enforcement suicide to line-of-duty death.
- Those affected by suicide. Family, friends, co-workers, the entire agency, and the community.
- The motivations for a law enforcement suicide. Critical incidents, relationship problems, substance abuse, to gain attention, to escape an intolerable situations, etc.
- Explore the *common myths* regarding suicide, such as it usually happens without warning, low risk after mood improvement,

once suicidal, always suicidal, intent on dying.
- The verbal and behavioral clues of suicide. I'm going to kill myself; I wish I were dead; you won't be seeing me any more; life has lost meaning; I can't take the pain; I'm really just getting tired of life. Comparing and contrasting the moods and behavior of the employee. Is he or she acting out of place as compared with usual conduct? Why is his or her work suddenly substandard? Why are they suddenly not getting along with co-workers? Temper outbursts or possible withdrawal.
- Major predictors of suicidal behavior include a prior suicide attempt, family history, a major relationship breakdown, internal investigation, focal point of a criminal investigation, the plan, availability of means, lethality of method.

INTERVENTION TACTICS

The police supervisor may well find himself or herself in a situation of having to intervene in the suicidal plans of a subordinate officer. The individual agency should have a plan in place to deal with an emergency employee–involved suicide intervention. This calls for ensuring that a mental health professional trained to treat police officers is continually available. The recommended intervention training of supervisors should at least contain the following elements:

- The process of the initial intervention such as remaining calm, assisting the employee in defining the problem, staying close, being an active listener, emphasizing the temporary nature of the problem, etc.
- Never sound shocked or offer empty promises, don't debate religion or morality, never leave the person alone.
- Important questions to ask during the intervention.

    1. Have you been thinking of hurting or killing yourself?
    2. How would you kill yourself?
    3. Have you attempted suicide before?
    4. Has anyone in your family attempted or committed suicide?
    5. What are the odds you will kill yourself?

6. What has been keeping you alive so far?
7. What do you think the future holds for you?

The briefly described training on suicide prevention and intervention is by no means all inclusive. There are many successful models of suicide prevention and intervention training. A critical emphasis when training law enforcement personnel in suicide prevention is the trust and credibility of the mental health professional instructor. Again, it is highly recommended that a trusted, veteran police officer team teach this block with the mental health professional.

CONCLUSION

There can be little argument the career choice of law enforcement carries with it an enhanced risk of suicide. This fact has been shown through a myriad of clinical studies. The first barrier that must be overcome in the prevention of police suicide is the police culture itself. Police officers are reluctant to seek psychological help for fear of being perceived as weak or possibly losing their jobs should department administration "find out." Law enforcement administrators have a responsibility to create an environment where training of all personnel in suicide prevention and intervention is the norm. Furthermore, in a profession filled with continual violence, death, and many other major stresses, departments must ensure competent and confidential mental health services are available for officers. To do anything less is irresponsible and uncaring. Baker (1996) states, "Police officers throughout the ranks must stop pretending that the problem of police suicide does not exist or that it will go away. Someone must break the silence of denial and take action. With further research, innovative prevention programs, and proactive training, officers lives can be saved."

REFERENCES

Baker, L. (1996). *Suicide is Greater Danger to Cops Than Homicide, UB Study Shows.* (Report No. 96/391). Buffalo, New York: University at Buffalo News.
Baker, T. (1996). *Preventing Police Suicide.* Text available at http://www.fbi.gov
Clark, D. (1998). *Suicide Prevention, Intervention and Postvention.* Handout at the

International Critical Incident Stress Foundation training, New Mexico.

Field, G. & Jones, C. (1999). Code of Silence Doesn't Help. June, 1A–2A. *USA Today.*

Kates, A. (1999). *Cop Shock.* Tucson: Holbrook Street Press.

Mitchell, J. (1990). *Emergency Services Stress.* New Jersey: Prentice Hall.

Turvey, B. (1997). *Police Officers: Control, Hopelessness And Suicide.* Los Angeles, California: Knowledge Solutions.

Violanti, J.M. (1996). *Police Suicide: Epidemic in Blue.* Springfield, IL: Charles C Thomas, Publisher.

Chapter 3

CLINICIANS, COPS, AND SUICIDE

DANIEL W. CLARK AND ELIZABETH K. WHITE

Is suicide within law enforcement a problem? Various sources report 300 completed police suicides annually (Thornton, 1998). Other sources report that a law enforcement officer (LEO) is more likely to die by suicide than by homicide. This reported suicide/homicide ratio ranges from 1.4 suicides per homicide to 8.2 suicides per homicide (Clark & White, 2000). However, these numbers and statistics are extremely difficult to prove.

Although we do not know the exact number of law enforcement officers who take their own lives every year, we believe that suicide within law enforcement is a significant problem. Each peace officer who commits suicide leaves behind family, partners, supervisors, and friends who are highly impacted.

In this chapter, we will focus on the clinical aspects of law enforcement suicide. We will explore issues such as why it is so difficult for LEOs to seek help, what family members, peers, and supervisors can do to help an officer who is considering suicide, plus what the police agency itself can do.

WHY IS IT SO DIFFICULT TO SEEK HELP?

Many factors may interfere with a LEO seeking help. Some of these factors are external to the LEO and stem from the culture within a law enforcement agency or the special requirements and expectations we, as a society, place on our peace officers. Some of these factors are internal personality traits or adaptations to being a peace officer. Awareness of these factors and agency intervention to counteract them can help peace officers receive the help they need when they need it.

Stigma of Suicide

Suicide is definitely a part of the law enforcement culture. Like domestic violence, suicide within the rank and file of law enforcement is a problem long hidden. Peace officers even have a slang reference for suicide–a peace officer "eats his or her gun." Yet, many departments maintain that they do not even keep records on completed suicides within their department.

Suzie Sawyer, the Executive Director of Concerns of Police Survivors, mailed 14,000 requests for information concerning surviving family members of officers who committed suicide to departments throughout the United States in 1995. She received only three responses (Violanti, Vena, & Marshall, 1996).

What is the message we are clearly sending our officers? "Don't talk about suicide!" Many peace officers still view suicide as disgraceful, cowardly, dishonoring, a weakness, or a failure. How likely is it that a peace officer will come forward to talk about something that is so clearly taboo and that may be generating considerable shame?

In the *A&E* video, "Cops on the Edge," retired officer Paul Ciurcina talks about his perception of how his fellow officers would respond if he told them he was suicidal. "They would tell me, 'you're crazy, you're not a cop, you're crazy. You don't belong on this job.' How could I go to somebody and say I'm gonna kill myself. What support would I get? Who would help me?"

Confidentiality Concerns

Many peace officers hesitate to seek help because of concerns about the confidentiality, or perceived lack thereof, of mental health treatment. Officers are fearful that their conversations will not remain confidential. Although part of this suspiciousness is likely to be job-related and based on old stories and rumors, there is sometimes a grain of truth in the old stories. Some mental health programs or sections may have a bad history of "leaking" information back to the agency.

Also, many agencies use psychologists for consultations on handling problem employees or for workplace violence assessment. This further muddies the water, because the "client" in these cases is the agency. A confidential relationship is not established with the employee. It is the responsibility of the psychologist to make sure all parties involved understand to what extent confidentiality does or does not exist. From the outside, however, this may appear as a psychologist collaborating with management to the detriment of an employee and may be perceived as a breach of confidentiality.

Officers sometimes feel safer seeking a mental health professional (MHP) from outside their agency, rather than using an in-house MHP or a MHP from the official Agency Employee Assistance Program/Service. But even this option is a two-edged sword. Many peace officers believe that an outside MHP, unless he or she has significant experience with law enforcement, will not understand the world of law enforcement. The outside MHP will not know the jargon or understand the "rules" that LEOs live by. The peace officer may therefore feel that he or she has no place to go when faced with overwhelming problems or feelings.

In addition, there is the confidentiality concern related to the outside world. Contact with a MHP creates a "medical record." There are some sticky legal questions regarding the content of mental health records. Allegations of wrongful death, excessive force, etc., often result in a plaintiff's attorney attempting to gain access to a peace officer's treatment records. Even in routine cases, LEOs may fear that prior psychological treatment will "get out" and be used to undermine their credibility in courtroom testimony.

Many of the current laws regarding confidentiality and legal privilege have sprung from cases involving law enforcement personnel. Treatment records are protected by federal law (and in most cases, state law as well). However, a judge may rule that the records are important to a case and demand that the records be released for an "in chambers" review. This is especially true if the peace officer has previously released his or her record by putting his or her mental status at question in a court of law—such as through a Workman's Compensation stress claim.

Job Impact Worries

Chief among the concerns, which inhibit LEOs from seeking

mental health assistance, is the fear that doing so will negatively impact their job. If it becomes known that they have sought mental health treatment, will their fitness for duty be questioned? Questions about their mental stability could have a negative impact on their ability to be promoted, as well as their ability to compete for special assignments, such as SWAT or training officer assignments.

The ultimate fear is that seeking mental health treatment will somehow cost them their job. This fear is pervasive: seeking mental health treatment may put your job at risk. Many state guidelines for peace officers include some language that states the person must be "free of mental or emotional problems" or free from "psychopathology" to be a sworn peace officer. Few employers other than law enforcement are allowed to place that kind of demand on their employees.

Fear of job loss, although traumatic for every person, can be particularly traumatic for peace officers that identify so strongly with their job. To most peace officers, being a cop is not only what they do but defines a large portion of who they are as a person. These fears, whether real or just perceived, can interfere with an LEO seeking assistance.

Personality Traits

We know that a certain type of person is drawn to a career in law enforcement. When they apply, applicants tend to be action oriented, problem-solving individuals who want to make a difference. During their career, they solve problems for others. It is a difficult mind shift for an officer to move from being a "problem solver" to a "problem haver."

We also know that many, if not most, peace officers develop a strong sense of personal invulnerability. Many people might describe officers as big, strong, tough, "supermen/women." Officers themselves often come to believe this pervasive stereotype. In fact, you may argue that officers need to have this mind-set to survive the streets. Thinking "it won't happen to me" becomes a psychological shield for many officers.

A mind-set of "problem solver" or "superman/woman" can actively interfere with a person seeking professional assistance when help is needed. The psychological shield of "invulnerability" can result in lack of preparedness should a crisis occur, denial of the problem, and delays in seeking help once a problem is identified.

Adaptations

We know that officers are flesh and blood just like everyone else. Brutal and bloody crime scenes, dead and dying children, senseless loss and violence all have an impact on our officers. Sometimes it is an immediate impact, whereas other times it accumulates over the course of their careers. Most peace officers develop the ability to shut off feelings to function on the job. Although this is a necessary part of how a peace officer copes with the day-to-day ugliness of law enforcement, it also can make him or her vulnerable to using this adaptation or coping mechanism too much.

A peace officer can become emotionally numb or cut off. The cost of such adaptations can range from irritability to sleep problems to medical problems. Many peace officers get referred to a MHP after a visit to the emergency department for a "heart attack," which turns out to be an anxiety attack. A peace officer may not correctly identify the problem as emotional and thus will not seek assistance from an MHP early on.

Because feelings are dealt with predominantly by shutting them down, a peace officer experiencing strong emotions that he or she cannot easily shut down can become overwhelmed and begin to have concerns about his or her sanity. This also can interfere with seeking assistance. "If I tell them what I am feeling, they will lock me up!"

The Stigma of Emotional Problems

Because the culture of law enforcement supports the personality traits and adaptations that LEOs make to cope with the job, peace officers often do not feel comfortable sharing concerns or feelings they may be having even with close friends or colleagues. Because most peace officers hide or shut down feelings, a LEO experiencing problems may feel isolated or defective—"nobody else is having a problem." He or she may be afraid to talk to colleagues for fear of being judged "out of control" or "crazy."

The Role of Alcohol

One of the few "coping tools" still somewhat condoned by law enforcement culture is alcohol. "Choir Practice," where colleagues meet after shift to drink and "decompress" from the job, is still alive and well in many agencies. Unfortunately alcohol, as a coping tool, leaves much to be desired. Alcohol increases feelings of depression and increases impulsivity. Alcohol is present in a large number of law enforcement suicides (White & Honig, 1999).

In addition, alcohol often brings more problems of its own such as marital difficulties, driving accidents (or arrests for driving under the influence), or medical complications. A peace officer who is possibly feeling suicidal because of life problems can quickly acquire a few more problems through the use or abuse of alcohol.

Mistrust of the Psychological Field

Often, the only contact a LEO has ever had with a psychologist is during a pre-employment psychological examination. Although relationships between law enforcement and psychologists have improved over the years, many LEOs still see psychologists as the people who get criminals off and who cannot seem to cure the severely mentally ill people that law enforcement must repeatedly deal with in the field. They may believe that "only crazy people" go to psychologists or other MHPs and that just talking to a MHP could not possibly help.

Medication as Treatment

Peace officers know that depression and suicidal ideation often lead to recommendations for taking "psychiatric" medications. Usually, the only experience a peace officer has had with drugs is contact with the addicts and dealers they arrest or the severely mentally ill individuals they must deal with in the field. Because most LEOs know very little about psychiatric medications, taking a drug to fix their emotions may seem a little too close to being a junky. Or, they may conclude that people who take drugs are really crazy, like the mentally ill individuals they see each day. Who would blame a peace officer for wanting to distance himself or herself from either of those two perceptions?

Peace officers may be concerned that the medication will make them feel out of control or in an "altered" state. They may also worry that the medication will degrade their job performance, impairing their judgment, decision-making skills, or reaction times. Remember, their only experience with these kinds of medications may be based solely on their contacts with the severely mentally ill.

With the advent of increased drug testing, many officers are concerned they may show up "hot" on a urinalysis because of taking medications. Although some agencies now have a urinalysis policy that states that prescription drugs (with proof of prescription) are not reported back to the agency, peace officers may not know their agency's policy or may fear it will not be respected.

In addition, many agencies have a policy that peace officers must report all medications they are taking. If the peace officer has chosen not to report that he or she is taking a psychotropic/psychiatric medication, the officer may face a new worry regarding a policy violation if the information gets back to his or her unit of assignment in any way. A peace officer may technically face disciplinary action for failing to report taking a medication, in addition to whatever reaction the agency may have to the fact that he or she is taking a psychotropic medication.

INTERVENTION

What Can a Colleague or Family Member Do?

"Just Listen"

Listening is a skill we often take for granted. You may have heard someone say, "just listen . . . ," implying that listening is an easy task. Far from it! Listening, and truly hearing another person is a very complex task.

The message conveyed when you truly listen to someone is "I care." I care enough to give you my attention. I care enough to respect what you are saying to me. I care about you. This can be a *very* powerful message, especially when the person may be feeling alone, isolated, hopeless, and like no one cares.

As you are listening to the person, stay calm. It is important that you not overreact to what they are sharing. Accept what they say as their view of what is happening around them. It does little good to argue with the person.

There are several phrases we recommend you avoid. The first is, "I know exactly how you feel." Even when said with positive intentions, this comment often evokes a strong negative response. Appropriately so, perhaps, because no one can know exactly how another feels. Try saying, "I can see how you might feel. . . ."

Second, avoid contradicting the person by saying "You don't mean that." The implied message is that you are not taking the person seriously. You are also calling the person a liar. Perhaps more appropriate would be, "I'm sorry that you are feeling so bad (low/unhappy/hopeless)."

Finally, avoid the clichés, "Don't worry–it will all work out" or "Everything will look better in the morning." You do not know that it will get better, so do not promise that it will get better. Offering appropriate hope can be very helpful but avoid promising something that you cannot deliver.

Understand the Mind-Set of Suicide

Suicide can be seen as a crisis in problem solving. The person has defined a problem for which suicide seems to be the best or, at times, the *only* solution. This mind-set can be called "tunnel vision." The person only sees a limited number of options, one of which is ending his or her own life. The person feels helpless and hopeless. They feel miserable and powerless to change the situation.

Once you understand the mind-set and the tunnel vision, a clear intervention is to help the person explore other options. If they are thinking in "black and white," a very common thought style in law enforcement, assist them in exploring the "gray areas."

Although other options are available, either the suicidal person has not considered them or has considered and rejected the other options. Therefore, help them brainstorm other possibilities and/or reconsider the options they rejected. Do they need to gather more information? Is there a way to modify the options they rejected to make those options more palatable to the person? Often, a helper makes the most difference by engendering new hope and by simply making the suicidal individual feel that she or he is no longer alone.

Seduction in the Line of Duty

Individuals contemplating suicide are sometimes held back by concerns about the impact on friends and family members—both emotional impact and functional impact (loss of a parent to a child, financial loss, etc.). This is especially true if children are involved. A suicidal person may feel a certain amount of anticipated shame and guilt for the damage that would be done and for how he or she would be viewed by loved ones. She or he may fear the religious consequences of a completed suicide.

It is important, therefore, to watch for another form of suicide among LEOs—that of an intentional line of duty death. Peace officers routinely face individuals who are more than willing to take the officer's life. Sometimes, the idea of a "suicide by suspect" may seem a more attractive way to end their pain. Rather than an action taken, it is an action not taken (e.g., failing to draw a weapon during a felony stop) that brings about death. The end result is the same, but the method of death and the responses to the death from friends, family, and employers are drastically different.

As we mourn the loss of life in a line of duty death, we often elevate the deceased to hero status. There are often memorials with hundreds or thousands of attendees. Emergency services people travel from all around the country, and even from outside the country, to attend the funeral. There is often a public outpouring of support for both the family and the agency.

When an officer dies by his or her own hand, however, there is often only private shame and guilt. The officer's family often reports feeling abandoned by the public and their agency. There is no outpouring of support or a large funeral.

If an officer is killed in the line of duty, the family receives federal and state death benefits. Although the money cannot bring their loved one back to life, the family can use these funds to cope with immediate expenses and ease the financial impact of the death.

When an officer dies by his or her own hand, there are no death benefits to the family. Their life insurance may or may not pay benefits, depending on the particular policy.

The seduction of a line of duty death becomes readily apparent when contrasted with suicide. The officer may begin taking unusual risks, may disregard officer safety procedures, or may engage in risky behaviors in an attempt to die in the line of duty, because they have decided that their family will be taken care of emotionally and financially, they will bring no shame or dishonor to their family or agency, and they can end their perceived pain.

Challenge Myths and Misconceptions

Many potential helpers are held back by various myths or misconceptions about suicide. You can never "give" somebody the idea of committing suicide; so asking does not endanger somebody's life. People who talk about suicide can and do go on to commit suicide; so take all talk seriously. Many people hesitate to take action, because they fear damaging the LEOs career. It is essential to remember that the consequences of seeking help are never as permanent as the consequences of suicide.

Asking the Question(s)

A major concern for most people when dealing with someone who may be suicidal is "How do I ask someone if they are suicidal?"

When asking about suicide, we recommend the straightforward approach. Ask them, "Are you thinking of hurting or killing yourself?" You are quite likely to get a straight answer to this straight question. This question also avoids any ambiguity, because you are clearly asking about suicide very openly. Avoid asking a leading question such as, "You aren't thinking of doing something stupid like suicide, are you?" Framed this way, the question obviously pulls for a "No!" answer, which may or may not be the truth.

A second major concern is "What do I do if they say YES?" For most people, the best answer is to get the person to a MHP for further assessment or to a hospital if the suicide seems imminent.

If you choose to refer the person to a MHP, please be careful whom you refer to. Try to refer the person to someone who understands the law enforcement culture. Too often, we hear about referrals "gone bad," in which the officer ends up suffering more than he or she was before the referral.

For instance, do not refer a cop to a child psychologist! Even a psychologist who specializes in seeing adults is not likely to understand the intricacies of law enforcement and may overreact to what they may hear from the officer, because some of things we discuss are not very pleasant.

Ideally, the agency will have a MHP on contract, in-house, or through an Employee Assistance Program/Service (EAP/EAS). There may also be a MHP associated with the Agency's Critical Incident Stress Management Team.

Alternative referrals can include anonymous suicide hotlines or crisis counseling lines. Although not sufficient for a person experiencing active suicidal ideation, referrals to peer support, chaplains, clergy, and self-help groups are all appropriate. Again, the agency or the agency's EAP should have lists of appropriate referral resources.

What Can a Supervisor Do?

Because most people do provide clues, either verbally or behaviorally, when they are contemplating suicide, a supervisor may be the first who sees or hears these clues. First-line supervisors are in a unique position to see behavior that may indicate a problem. Supervisors, therefore, have all the responsibilities of colleagues and more.

It is essential that supervisors know their troops. Knowing what is normal or abnormal for any particular officer can often be the basis for spotting a LEO in trouble. Supervisors must be familiar with the general signs and symptoms of emotional problems and of individuals in crisis. Supervisors must be thoroughly versed in risk indicators for suicide and should know agency policy should they suspect a person is suicidal. Supervisors should be aware of available resources and the means for activating these resources.

One of the most crucial jobs of the supervisor is to create an environment where a LEO feels that problems will be met with nonjudgmental support, active listening, and problem solving rather than knee-jerk reactivity and punitive action.

What Can a Mental Health Professional Do?

Therapy

Remember that we are operating in crisis mode when someone is acutely suicidal. The focus needs to be on the immediate situation, the individual's feelings, and the support resources the therapist and/or individual can rally on his or her behalf. The role of the MHP at this point is to be active, goal-oriented, and specific. An excellent resource for both assessment and intervention techniques is Shawn Shea's book, *The Practical Art of Suicide Assessment: A Guide for Mental Health Professionals and Substance Abuse Counselors* (1999).

The first step in intervention after determining that this individual is considering suicide is assessing the risk level. Where is this person on a suicide risk continuum? Are they "imminently suicidal?" Are they thinking about ending their life? If so, how strong are these feelings, and how often do they occur?

Details an MHP needs to determine include does the person have a prior history or a family history of suicidal behavior? Do they have a plan? How specific, lethal, and available is the method they have chosen? How detailed is the plan? The more detailed the plan is, the higher the risk.

What resources does the individual have available? Resources may include family, friends, co-workers, clergy, PSPs, physicians, therapists, etc. MHPs want to help the person rally the resources or the support system.

The MHP may be part of that support system. During the crisis period, there should be frequent contact, either in person or by a phone call. As the crisis recedes, the MHP will step down the frequency of contact and gradually shift the focus from immediate needs to longer term coping skills and underlying causes for the suicidal thoughts and feelings.

Medications

Medication is a viable option for LEOs experiencing depression and/or suicidal ideation. Recent advances in psychopharmacology have resulted in antidepressant medications that can break the chokehold of hopelessness and helplessness without causing side effects that interfere with the performance of police functions. It is essential that LEOs be evaluated for medication by medical professionals who understand the job requirements of a peace officer and who choose medications accordingly. LEOs may need more detailed explanations of side effects plus additional assistance understanding the action and role of an antidepressant to overcome concerns about the use of psychotropic medications.

Because LEOs are often action-oriented individuals, it is particularly important to explain the time delay in the effectiveness of antidepressant medications. Because depression often represents a deficit in the brain of certain necessary chemicals, it takes time for the medication to assist the body in accumulating more of those chemicals. An analogy would be that an antidepressant can put the plug in the bathtub drain, but it will still take awhile for the natural inflow of water to refill the tub. It may be 7–10 days before a person experiences noticeable improvement in symptoms or feelings. Supportive action will be crucial during that time to help the LEO tolerate the delay.

During this "waiting period," the LEO may actually be at greater risk for suicide. Often individuals who are depressed have so little energy, even the act of suicide is beyond them. Antidepressant medications help restore sleep and may increase energy. If the person is not in supportive therapy, this increase in energy can result in an actual suicide attempt before the improvement in mood and hope takes effect.

Weapons Removal

More than 80 percent of law enforcement officers use a handgun to commit suicide. A simplistic suicide intervention plan would be to remove their duty weapon. No gun—no suicide, right?

A significant problem with this strategy, however, is that removing a LEO's gun removes his or her ability to work. Although it is logical that a person who is imminently suicidal should not be at work, many individuals experience intermittent suicidal ideation or ideation that is not persistent or intense enough to warrant such drastic actions. Many MHPs remove access to weapons as an automatic safeguard at the first sign of any suicidal feelings. The person's employer need never know. This conservative action is more problematic with law enforcement. An alternative action appropriate to law enforcement may be to remove access to firearms when off duty. A duty weapon can be kept at work. Personal weapons may be secured with friends or by the law enforcement psychologist (if he or she has appropriate storage security). Another option is for the peace officer to take vacation time, leaving their weapons with a friend or a law enforcement psychologist. This avoids the embarrassment and stigma of publicly turning in weapons to the agency.

If a LEO is imminently suicidal and should not have access to firearms, it is important to remember that most of officers can readily access more than one gun. Many carry a backup weapon on their person, in the glove box or trunk of the car, and/or in their locker. Many are avid hunters and outdoorsmen or women.

Although removing the chosen means of suicide is an accepted intervention with the general public, it may not be effective with law enforcement or military personnel. Removing the duty weapon may seem to solve the problem, but it only solves the immediate problem. If you remove the primary weapon, the officer may simply use a backup.

Another concern is the importance or the meaning of the weapon to police and military personnel. They view their weapon as much more than merely a means to protect themselves. Their weapon is often seen as a symbol of their authority. Their weapon also declares their identification as a law enforcement officer or military member. Even more important, however, may be the psychological shield the weapon represents. The MHP must address with the peace officer the impact and likely emotional reactions to such an event (whether implemented by the Agency or in an informal agreement with the MHP).

Although removing a weapon may be a necessary action for an imminently suicidal individual, removing a weapon from a LEO has additional complications and ramifications that must be considered before such an action is taken.

Hospitalization

MHPs try to reserve hospitalization as a last resort, particularly involuntary hospitalization. One of the most drastic actions that can be taken regarding a potentially suicidal person is to contact 911 to involuntarily hospitalize him or her. The person(s) who responds to a 911 call of this nature is usually another officer and possibly a paramedic or mental health evaluation team of some kind. Thus, the officer's employer is often fully aware of what has happened.

Even if the officer lives outside the jurisdiction of his or her employer, most agencies will notify the employing agency as a courtesy when one of their personnel is brought to the attention of law enforcement. Even if the person is not subsequently hospitalized, the damage may have already been done. Again the officer is at risk for significant job impact in terms of damaged reputation, being relieved of duty, and having his or her career impacted in terms of promotion or specialty assignments in the future.

In addition, clinicians need to be aware of local laws regarding weapons possession. According to California state law, if an individual is involuntarily hospitalized for risk to self (Health & Welfare code 5150), that individual may not carry or purchase a firearm for five years. Although any clinician would probably argue that a person who must be involuntarily hospitalized should not be carrying a firearm, would that clinician say that the same would be true a year later or two years later?

In California, an involuntary hospitalization means the peace officer may be terminated from his or her current employment and may be unable to work in law enforcement for five years. In all honesty, short of a court appeal, the officer's career may have ended. Although many individuals may incur job consequences after a hospitalization caused by time lost from work or possible stigma, the impact on a law enforcement officer is much greater.

Voluntary hospitalizations, however, may not have such a drastic impact on a career. Arrangements may be quietly made, on a need-to-know basis, so the officer can receive the help he or she needs.

What Can The Agency Do?

Peer Support/Certified Incident Stress Management Programs

Both authors strongly endorse peer support programs. We know that police officers in crisis, if they are going to talk with anyone, will probably first choose another officer to confide in. A trained peer support person (PSP) is on scene, has already established credibility, and is often more easily accepted by the LEO than a MHP.

The Police Psychological Services Section of the International Association of Chiefs of Police defines the goal of a peer support program as "the opportunity to receive emotional and tangible peer support through times of personal or professional crises and to help anticipate and address potential difficulties."

An active Peer Support Program may serve two functions. First, PSPs can help those officers who are unwilling to seek help from MHPs. Unfortunately, some officers do not trust MHPs, especially "in-house" MHPs. They may see MHPs as providing "false, paid friendship" (Allen, 1986). PSPs, on the other hand, often have the "been there–done that" badge of experience.

Second, PSPs may provide a link or a bridge to the MHP. One of the most potent referrals someone can give is to say, "I've talked to this man/woman, and they're OK." In our peer support training courses, both authors stress the importance of effective and timely referrals to MHPs, when necessary.

A PSP is similar to a friend or family member who provides support. However, a PSP has additional training in responding to individuals with suicidal ideation and is more aware of resources available in the community and in the agency they both serve.

Ideally, a Peer Support Program is part of an overall Critical Incident Stress Management (CISM) program within the agency. An effective CISM program will offer preincident education, peer support, critical incident stress debriefings, family debriefings, etc. CISM has been shown to mitigate the impact of stress and critical incident stress within the emergency services.

Affirmative Command Messages

As stated previously, one of the most prevalent and damaging myths about mental health services is that seeking help will cost officers their jobs. Many officers view seeking help as a sign of weakness or inferiority. They look around and see "everyone else" apparently handling stress with no problem.

Supervisors and the chain of command can dispel this myth by assuring officers that seeking help is a sign of strength, not weakness. Seeking help can be a step toward becoming a better officer. This philosophy must trickle down from above and be endorsed by command staff, as well as line supervisors.

Consider the problem-solving paradigm: "define a problem, find a solution, and implement the solution." This paradigm can be easily applied to seeking mental health support. However, it is the chain of command's responsibility to change the perception that seeking help will automatically cost the officer his or her job. This change in perception is brought about by training supervisors and by the creation of policy, which ensures that individuals seeking help are handled respectfully and supportively.

One way for the chain of command to reinforce the message that seeking help is "Okay" is to ensure that mental health services are competent and readily available. A second means is to ensure that receiving help is completely confidential. Cops are notoriously skeptical and cynical. It is often difficult for them to trust people. A sure way to kill any mental health program's effectiveness is for it to gain a reputation for not keeping confidential information confidential. Both the agency and the MHPs must keep this firmly in mind.

The command structure's support for the Peer Support and CISM programs can send the message that their officers have resources, if they choose to use them. One of the authors used the message "You are not alone"–coupled with a list of local resources and phone numbers during the holiday season to effectively send the message that there are many resources available.

An affirmative command message can also be conveyed by how a completed suicide is handled by the agency. A respectful, nonjudgmental handling of a completed suicide may lead others who are contemplating suicide to believe that help is available.

Training Issues–Cadets

Another effective tool for the agency is training. Many of the concerns we raise may be addressed through training, either as cadets or through periodic unit level/in-service training.

First, we recommend that suicide awareness training be part of the core curriculum taught to new cadets. Within this training, both awareness of suicidal indicators and possible basic interventions must be covered. Myths or misinformation that the cadets may have must be challenged and corrected. Encourage attendees to take all suicidal statements and threats seriously. Cadets must also be made aware of the truth regarding confidentiality concerns and job impact realities. All the blocks to seeking help described earlier should be identified and dealt with during the training.

Second, as discussed earlier, affirm that seeking mental health support may be viewed as a strength and not a weakness. Stress the importance of assisting others to seek help also. Introduce the concept that "watching each other's backs" goes beyond physical protection and should include emotional support and assistance.

Third, the training must identify sources of help available to the officers and the means to access them 24 hours a day. This may include an Employee Assistance Program/Service, an in-house or contracted psychologist, or other MHPs. If a Peer Support or Critical Incident Team is available, ensure the attendees know how to reach those teams.

A useful activity during a suicide awareness and intervention class can be developing a list of available resources. One of the authors uses a three-ringed bulls eye, which the class fills in using local resources. The inner ring lists 24-hour resources, the middle ring lists professional resources, and the outer ring lists community resources. At the completion of the exercise, the class has typically listed approximately 30 helping resources available in their local and extended area.

Finally, teach effective stress management techniques. As part of the instruction, emphasize that police work is inherently stressful, and exposure to trauma is inevitable. It is essential that cadets lay the groundwork for successful stress coping before leaving the academy. Trying to develop good stress coping while in the middle of a crisis is unrealistic at best.

Training Issues–Supervisors

It is essential that supervisors not only receive a refresher course regarding the basics of signs and symptoms of suicide, but that they also are knowledgeable about available resources, contact procedures, and appropriate policy and procedures for handling employees in crisis. Many line staff dismiss training about suicide because of an "it will never happen to me" attitude. Because a line supervisor will be responsible for a number of subordinates, she or he cannot afford such an attitude. It will happen!

Training for supervisors must be hands on, using practical application techniques such as role playing and scenario exercises to help hone supervisory skills. Supervisors must be aware of appropriate actions to take and must be sensitive to confidentiality issues.

Information regarding emotional difficulties of subordinates must be kept on a strictly need-to-know basis.

It is particularly important that supervisors be aware of their own beliefs, biases, and misinformation about suicide, because these will color how they respond to a LEO in trouble.

Intervention–Summary

Many peace officers fear that if they mention suicide, they will be involuntarily hospitalized and lose their job. However, as we have pointed out previously, there are many options available before we as MHPs even consider involuntary hospitalization.

Figure 3.1 is an example of necessary and sufficient intervention. Peace officers understand the continuum for the use of force. This figure is a comparable "use of intervention" continuum. Intervention often starts with peers or family members. Many individuals respond very well to intervention at this level. For those who

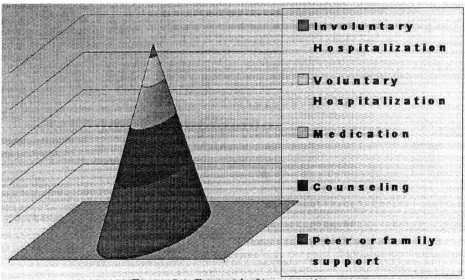

Figure 3.1. Pyramid of intervention.

need additional assistance, counseling with a mental health professional is the next level of intervention. At times, some individuals may benefit from a temporary course of medication, the next level of care.

In some circumstances, the individual may feel so badly about his or her life, so out of control, that hospitalization may be the best option. However, before we reach this final level of intervention, the impact of voluntary vs. involuntary hospitalization on a LEO's career must be considered.

Most agencies, and the legal system, look differently at voluntary vs. involuntary hospitalization. The former is a problem-solving approach: define a problem (considering suicide), define a solution (voluntary hospitalization), and implement the solution. The latter is a choice forced on the person. At least in California, the latter carries a stiff consequence: prohibition from owning a firearm for five years. Voluntary hospitalization does not provoke such a consequence. Involuntary hospitalization should, therefore, be reserved for only those rare circumstances in which no other option is feasible.

CONCLUSION

The issue of suicide within a law enforcement environment poses additional problems and pitfalls not present when dealing with other populations. Law enforcement professionals face additional obstacles to seeking the assistance they may need.

The first step in overcoming these obstacles is awareness and understanding. The agency can and should attempt to overcome these obstacles through a mind-set that emphasizes acceptance and support for those officers who self-identify as having emotional problems, up to and including suicidal ideation. Education, at both the line staff and supervisor level, will play a key role in this endeavor. Training must target identified obstacles, be they internal to the person or related to the law enforcement culture and environment.

The second step is active intervention. All members of the law enforcement family play a role in intervention, be they family, colleagues, supervisors, agencies, or mental health professionals who provide assistance to law enforcement personnel.

Last, an agency can and should ensure that competent, confidential services are available at all times to a peace officer in trouble. MHPs, chaplains, and peer supporters can provide critical support to an officer in need.

The impact of suicide on a law enforcement population is wide-

spread and devastating. And although suicide may never be elim-
inated, awareness and timely intervention can definitely reduce its
likelihood.

REFERENCES

Allen, S.W. (1986). Suicide and indirect self-destructive behavior among police. In
    J.T. Resse & H.A. Goldstein (Eds.), *Psychological Services for Law Enforcement* (pp.
    413-417). Washington, DC: U.S. Government Printing Office.
Clark, D.W. & White, E.K. (2000, April). *Law Enforcement Suicide: An Inside Look.*
    Paper presented at the 33rd Annual American Association of Suicidology
    Conference, Los Angeles, California.
Shea, S. (1999) *The Practical Art of Suicide Assessment: A Guide for Mental Health
    Professionals and Substance Abuse Counselors.* N.Y.: Wiley & Sons.
Thornton, K. (1998, August 27). Police captain's suicide part of painful trend. Rate
    much higher among law officers. *The Boston Globe.*
Violanti, J.M., Vena, J.E., & Marshall, J.R. (1996). Suicides, homicides, and acci-
    dental death: A comparative risk assessment of police officers and municipal
    workers. *American Journal of Industrial Medicine, 30,* 99–104.
White, E.K. & Honig, A.L. (1999, October). *Death by Their Own Hand: Have
    We Failed to Protect Our Protectors?* Paper presented at the 106th Annual
    International Association of Chiefs of Police Conference, Charlotte, North
    Carolina.

Chapter 4

QPR: POLICE SUICIDE PREVENTION

PAUL QUINNETT AND VICKIE M. WATSON

A 5-year veteran uniformed police officer, in acute distress about his wife divorcing him, hints to his shift supervisor, "Forget that transfer I asked for; I've decided to work things out permanently."

The shift supervisor takes him aside and asks, "What's the matter? Is something going on in your personal life?"

After this inquiry, the officer announces that his wife is leaving him, describes his sense of devastation, and laments his inability to reverse her decision.

The supervisor says, "I'm worried about you and concerned for your safety. Have you had any thoughts about killing yourself?" The officer nods.

"Then I want you to see a professional immediately—strictly confidential. I'll make arrangements. Chaplain or psychologist?"

"Psychologist," the officer replies, accepting help. Then he asks, "Do I have to give up my badge and gun?"

"No," replies the supervisor. "But for your safety you have to promise me you will not kill yourself until you've gotten some help. Are you willing to do that?"

"Okay," the officer sighs. "Okay, okay. . . . How soon can I see the psychologist?"

"Today. I will take you myself," replies the supervisor.

Suicide is a tragedy that impacts tens of thousands of people each year: family members, friends and colleagues. Suicide also has an impact on those in law enforcement, whether as direct observers of a death by suicide, as survivors of a family member or friend's suicide, or as a person struggling with his or her own personal thoughts of self-destruction. The fact is we expect a lot of law enforcement personnel and they, in turn, expect a lot of themselves. The weight of the badge is heavier than many realized when they initially entered this profession. As stated by Sergeant Bryan Skinner, "Being a police officer is not something I do, but something I am" (Skinner, 1994).

The weight of the badge *can* also weigh heavily on family members. When men and women take up this profession of serving the public, they are inadvertently choosing a lifestyle fraught with responsibility, stress, exposure to trauma, isolation, and a constant need to be in emotional control. Balancing all the various roles and emotions can be difficult. Posttraumatic stress disorder (PTSD), depression, alcohol abuse, and relationship problems are all too often unhealthy consequences of this profession. Unfortunately, so, too, is suicide.

With only one hour of training, police officers and others can be taught to make more effective interventions in the suicidal crisis of another individual. Because of this one-hour training, the supervisor in the preceding interaction was able to apply a direct and effective suicide intervention. Called QPR, the intervention consists of three bold steps: *questioning* the meaning of possible suicidal communications, *persuading* the person in crisis to accept help, and *referring* the person to the appropriate resource.

Whether a supervisor, colleague, or friend, the fact is that we are all in a position to potentially make a difference in the life of a suicidal person. If we are to make such a difference, each of us must be willing to take action. That action may be directed at people close to us or in interactions with members of the larger community. The important thing to remember is that taking action can and does help save lives.

BACKGROUND

In taking steps to make a difference, it is important to realize that the supervisor in the opening scenario did all the right things at the right time. Because of the supervisor's interventions, the officer provided a good faith promise not to kill himself and received the necessary professional help immediately, resulting in a positive outcome.

Typical of most suicidal crises, the nature of the officer's troubles took a long time to develop but seemed brief, transient, and remedial during the crisis itself. A timely and caring discussion about his hinted plan to commit suicide ("I've decided to work things out permanently"), together with an immediate referral, enabled this officer to receive the counseling necessary to prevent a suicide attempt. This officer weathered his emotional storm and returned to duty in a few days with his pride and self-esteem intact. Many face similar emotional storms in life. Too often in the past, those in key positions to help have either not known what to do or were incapacitated by a lack of information about suicide and its nature and did not have the confidence to act. Fortunately, times are changing, as is the willingness to get involved in the lives of potentially suicidal persons.

Three things happened in the scenario with the officer to help avert a possible tragedy, not only for the officer and his family, but for the department as well. First, the supervisor recognized that the officer's struggle with depression and suicide was not about a "good officer gone bad," a powerful title used by Gene Sanders, Ph.D. in an article looking at PTSD issues for police officers (Sanders, 1999). Rather, the supervisor recognized an individual in distress and implemented effective skills in suicide prevention. These same skills could just as easily have been used with a family member, a friend, or a citizen in distress.

Second, the supervisor acted immediately, with courage. He also offered strong support. Too often, those close to the individual contemplating suicide respond to suicidal communications with denial, fear, avoidance, and passivity. No matter how unintended, this type of response often heightens the sufferer's sense of isolation, helplessness, and hopelessness.

Third, immediate support was offered to the officer in the form of a mental health resource person and/or a trained chaplain. Having ready access to a safe, tolerant, and helpful professional often reduces the customary resistance that many officers, and others, feel when outside help is needed. The supervisor's willingness to accompany the officer to the initial appointment was also a form of support and likely increased the officer's willingness to follow through with the scheduled appointment.

SUICIDE RESEARCH

No matter what our occupation, no one is immune to everyday struggles and/or psychological difficulties. Some occupations are actually associated with an increased likelihood of experiencing such stress-related problems. At present, law enforcement is one of those higher risk professions. Perhaps this is because of the stress of the job itself. Maybe it relates to the high standards that officers often place on themselves and, into the bargain, the high standards of service they provide to the public they serve. Regardless, too many law enforcement officers lives, and the lives of family members and friends, are impacted each year as a result of the emotional storm within and the suicidal journey that ensues.

Although statistics remain limited, law enforcement personnel have been found to be overrepresented in the suicide data. Violanti, in his book *Police Suicide: Epidemic in Blue*, reported that "Overall, police officers had an increased relative risk for suicide over all types of death in comparison to municipal worker Suicide may thus be considered a potentially higher risk to officers when compared to other hazards of policing and other occupations" (Violanti, 1996). Data suggest a sad, but steady, trend in which more officers lose their lives each year to suicide than to homicide. In a survey of the Nation's largest police departments, *USA Today* (Field & Jones, 1999) reported that:

- In New York, 36 officers were killed in violent confrontations with suspects from 1985–1999. During the same time period, 87 officers took their own lives.
- In Los Angeles, 11 officers were slain while on duty from 1989–1999. Twenty killed themselves.
- In Chicago, 12 officers were slain while on duty between 1990 and 1999. Twenty-Two officers killed themselves during that same time period.
- The FBI lost four special agents in the line of duty since 1993. Eighteen special agents killed themselves (during comparable

years of 1993–1999.)

- The U.S. Customs Service lost seven agents to suicide in 1998 alone.
- Some research shows that the suicide rate of officers is roughly three times the national average (Baker & Baker, 1996; Hill & Clawson, 1998). Another researcher reported that the suicide rate among police officers doubled from 1950–1990 (Violanti, 1995). Considering the emotional wreckage suicides cause in the community for friends, colleagues, and family members, even a single suicide by a law enforcement officer is one too many.

Although research literature on suicide and its prevention has grown slowly because of a lack of funding, it is important to note that steady progress is being made. Researchers know a great deal more today than they knew ten years ago about the medical and psychological conditions under which people consider suicide. Among the information learned recently:

- Suicidal crises tend to be short, not long.
- Most suicides are completed by people with untreated clinical depression, often precipitated by chronic stress and complicated by acute or chronic alcohol intoxication.
- If treated aggressively, 70 percent of depressed, suicidal people will respond favorably to treatment in a matter of a few weeks.
- The newer antidepressant medications cause few side effects that impair job or family functioning and, as a result, compliance with medication regimens results in excellent treatment responses (Ward, 1997).

THE SUICIDAL JOURNEY

Although some suicidal acts are impulsive, most of suicidal persons follow a known psychological route: from idea to act. Most American adults only think about suicide and never act on their thoughts. The act of suicide may or may not be fatal, but it is important to remember that the journey begins with the idea that suicide will solve all of one's problems and will bring an end to one's mental anguish and suffering. Suicide may also be seen as a way to escape an intolerable situation.

Once a person considers suicide, the notion may be discarded as a

Figure 4.1
Suicidal Crisis Episode

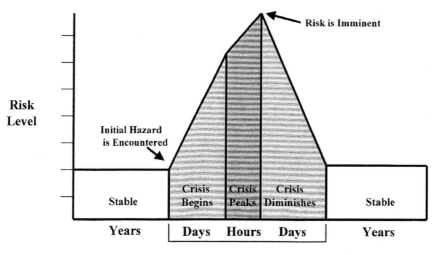

bad idea or, if relief is not forthcoming, the journey to suicide may continue onward. If it continues, the increasingly suicidal person must find a time, place, and means to make an attempt. The journey may be short or long. Sometimes the journey takes only hours, but typically it takes a matter of weeks or even years. For most people, the "hot phase" of a suicide crisis begins and ends within approximately three weeks.

If help arrives in time, and before a suicide attempt is made, most lives can be saved. More than one reader of this book has likely already saved one or more lives from suicide by intervening in the journey to self-destruction.

METHODS OF SUICIDE

As part of the journey, people contemplating suicide must make a decision about the method they intend to use to bring about death. This decision almost always reflects the person's values, identity, training, and/or the availability of the selected method. Thus, anesthesiologists tend to use drugs, pilots may use an aircraft, and law enforcement officers most frequently will use a firearm, as do most Americans. Self-inflicted gunshot wounds have been the leading cause of death by suicide for both men and women in the United States for several decades, and firearms are now the method most chosen by American teenagers (McIntosh, 1998). Unlike other less-lethal methods with which one may attempt suicide, the use of a firearm provides little opportunity for rescue, resuscitation, or second chances. According to some research, not only do police officers overwhelmingly select firearms as their method of suicide, but they experience a 6.4 greater risk of dying by a self-inflicted gunshot than people in other occupations (Violanti, Vena, & Marshall, 1996).

THE NATURE OF SUICIDAL COMMUNICATIONS

The success of the QPR method hinges on the fact that those considering suicide generally tell someone, either by word or deed, what they plan to do before they do it. This interpersonal communication functions as a window of opportunity for people in contact with the person contemplating suicide to intervene by acting boldly to stop the suicidal journey.

Unpublished research from the U.S. Department of the Navy found that among 41 completed suicides, 90 percent of those who took their lives communicated their intentions before their deaths (Anjeski, 1996). In 66 percent of these cases, the person directed suicidal communications to a shipmate, spouse, family member, or significant other. Unfortunately, an opportunity to query potentially suicidal *persons* occurred in only 34 percent of these cases when, according to the records, these *sailors* had contact with clergy or professional healthcare providers. These data suggest there may have been many "missed opportunities" to interrupt suicidal journeys already in progress and to make appropriate interventions and referrals.

Suicidal communications or clues most frequently fit into four basic categories: direct verbal, indirect verbal, behavioral, and situational. Direct verbal communications are relatively easy to understand and do not require special listening skills or interpretive powers. "I'm going to shoot myself" is easy enough to understand. However, if an intervention is to be successful, appropriate and supportive action is required *at the time the communication is sent.* We have an old saying in suicide prevention, "Whatever you do, do *something!*"

One experienced sheriff advised that when he was in the acute phase of his one and only suicide crisis, he drove up to an old friend having coffee in his patrol car. When his friend rolled down the window, the sheriff said, "I'm going to kill myself tomorrow." His friend stared at him in apparent disbelief, rolled up his window, and drove off. Fortunately, the officer survived his crisis.

All suicidal communications are not as direct and easily interpreted as illustrated in the preceding example. Because potential rescuers may reject direct communication about suicidal intent, suicidal persons frequently revert to what are called "coded clues" or "hints" that they may be considering suicide. These indirect verbal threats may be more challenging to interpret, but they can be understood, especially with a little training. The statement, "I'm going to eat my gun." says nothing about suicide per se, but anyone familiar with firearms knows what this means. An even more subtle example of an indirect clue can found in a recent mystery novel involving police officers as the central characters. The book *Red Light* by T. Jefferson Parker describes a scene in which two officers investigating a murder are discussing the fact that the wife of one of the partners is dying of a brain tumor. "Fly away, fly away. . . . That's what I'm good for. When this is over (meaning his wife's death), I'll do it." In this excerpt, the police officer is giving an indirect or *coded* suicidal communication. The initial response of his female partner is to think "It seemed a witless invasion to ask, '*What will you do?*'" Yet, the novel reflects that she clearly knew what was being communicated. Fortunately, the female partner quickly contacts a psychiatrist friend, shares her concerns, is reminded of risk factors and clues of police officers considering suicide, and is encouraged to actively intervene using the skills she learned at a QPR training several months earlier (Parker, 2000). Is this recently published novel written for purposes of entertainment? Yes. But, is it also a reflection of a

Figure 4.2
Suicidal Clues and Warning Signs

Direct Verbal Clues

- "I wish I were dead."
- "I've decided to kill myself."
- "I'm going to end it all."
- "If (such and such) doesn't happen, I'll kill myself."
- "I'm going to commit suicide."

Behavioral Clues

- Donating body to medical school
- Changes in behavior (especially episodes of yelling or hitting, throwing things, or failing to get along with family, friends, and peers)
- Sudden interest or disinterest in religion
- Relapse into drug or alcohol use, especially after a period of recovery

Indirect, or Coded, Verbal Clues

- "I'm tired of life."
- "My family would be better off without me."
- "Nobody needs me anymore."
- "Sometimes the thought of eating my gun doesn't seem like such a bad idea."
- "It was good at times, but we must all say goodbye sometime."
- "Here, take this (cherished possession); I won't be needing it anymore."

Situational Clues

- Sudden rejection by a loved one (e.g., girlfriend or boyfriend), or an unwanted separation or divorce
- Recent move—especially if it is unwanted
- Death of a spouse, child, or friend (with increased risk if death is by suicide)
- Diagnosis of a terminal illness
- Sudden, unexpected loss of freedom (e.g., about to be arrested, pending time in prison, etc.)
- Anticipated loss of financial security
- Publicly humiliating event or situation of feeling a "loss of face"

---

very real situation that could be encountered? Most definitely.

Men may sometimes also make what are called "dire predictions." Before to his death, one man made the statement to his wife after she filed for divorce, "You will find a dead man in a car in front of the house." Another man stated to his doctor, "Don't worry about me, I'll be six feet under next week." These "dire predictions" related to specifically to the intent of these men to kill themselves—and both did.

Individuals in a suicidal crisis do not always verbally communicate their intentions but rather may act out their distress. Engagement in these behaviors could indicate a plan to end their lives. These behavioral clues may be difficult at times to interpret, in part because there can be several different reasons for their occurrence. Behavioral clues include making a will, giving away prized possessions, stopping church attendance, or making funeral arrangements. When combined with possible verbal clues, or even a strong "gut reaction" that something is amiss, these behavioral clues can be part of an overall picture of despondency and potential suicidal considerations.

Finally, it is important to realize that "suicidal situations" are not communications but an acute stress context in which an individual feels caught up in a web of seemingly impossible circumstances for which suicide becomes an acceptable solution. For example, best friends since elementary school, two 13-year-old boys start high school together. Two weeks later, one of the boys is struck and killed by a drunk driver. Feeling depressed and isolated, and maybe never having experienced the death of someone close to him before, the young man left behind may begin to view suicide as the only answer for coping with his pain and loss. In his mind, he may also see his own death as a way of rejoining or being with his friend. Developmental considerations, experience in coping with past loss or trauma, the amount of social or professional support available, etc. all contribute to the equation of risk and need to be addressed.

For law enforcement personnel, a fear of public exposure following an arrest or the threat of an investigation that may lead to arrest or negative public attention creates a special crisis situation in which no face-saving exit may appear open. In these circumstances, suicide may seem to be the only way out. Any time a senior member of the force, a high-ranking officer or anyone who wears the uniform is about to be exposed in the media for criminal behavior or otherwise humiliated in public, aggressive outreach and intervention is recommended.

LAW ENFORCEMENT APPLICATIONS

QPR has particular application to law enforcement environments, both within a department and through Employee Assistance Programs (EAPs). The nature of close-knit associations and the necessity of teamwork make the training of officers in QPR a necessity. It is often co-workers on the force who may be in the most likely position to see warning signs of risk that could lead to a life-saving intervention. Similarly, spouses and family members may pick up on different clues. More opportunities for early intervention exist when members of a socially integrated organization (including families) are trained to recognize a potential suicide crisis in progress and are trained in what steps to take to interrupt the suicidal journey.

QPR, like cardiopulmonary resuscitation (CPR) for emergency medical interventions, is also very applicable within the broader community setting. Officers respond on a regular basis to calls of violence, substance use or abuse, suicide, and homicide. Many of these calls have, at their root, a distressed individual who may be feeling hopeless and questioning whether his or her life is worth living. Our increasing awareness of the phenomenon referred to as "suicide by cop" is but one other example. Although the "relationship" between the police officer and community member may be a new one, the possibility of successful intervention still exists and the method of QPR can be easily be applied.

In the same way a homicide requires opportunity (some experts have referred to suicide as homicide in the 180th degree), so too, does a suicide. Distressed individuals often create this opportunity by picking a fight with a friend, avoiding colleagues, resigning from the department ball team, engaging in increased alcohol use, or withdrawing from the very people who might help them survive. Police officers, and those who work with them, must raise their own awareness about the depth and breadth of this problem and learn to recognize that social withdrawal may be a sign that something is seriously wrong. The more people who know what to do and when to do it, the tighter the suicide prevention safety network becomes, and the better the chances that any given individual caught up in a personal crisis can survive that crisis.

With very few exceptions, most people caught up in a crisis situation will benefit from counseling, even when the problems driving the crisis threaten their careers and futures. This is true of law enforcement personnel as well the general public. QPR proves especially helpful in environments where individuals at risk are unlikely to seek assistance on their own, because they believe that voluntarily seeking mental health care may result in public shame or could damage their careers.

Because of the reticence to seek help, a mild depression may become a serious and debilitating one. The person may turn to alcohol use as one means of coping with their distress or symptoms of depression, thus seriously impairing their judgment. The person in crisis may also become more irritable or angry and withdraw from those who could help. Unfortunately, these "coping strategies" only tend to make matters worse and, unless early detection and referrals are made, may require formal disciplinary actions.

By reducing the stigma of mental health treatment, counseling, and expanding the pool of properly trained individuals so that effective, officer-friendly mental health services are more readily available, positive changes are possible. If necessary, a direct order to seek counseling is better than doing nothing. Doing nothing may be interpreted by the potentially suicidal person as not caring or confirmation that life is, in fact, just as hopeless as they currently perceive it to be.

Another reason associated with the elevated risk for suicide may be the tendency for law enforcement personnel to be reluctant to seek help voluntarily or in a timely fashion. This can be true, to a lesser degree, for the rest of the population as well, but the hesitance seems to occur with even greater prevalence among police and sheriff's department officers. Unfortunately, if suffering from stress-induced depression, the psychological condition of suicidal people tends to worsen over time and leads, in some cases, to a sense of utter hopelessness that clouds their thinking. When added to the well-documented risk factors of being a white, black, or Hispanic male (National Center for Health Statistics, 1996) and working in a high-stress environment that requires access to a firearm, a potentially toxic psychosocial formula for personal disaster exists.

Similar characteristics can be true of the impact of the officer's stress on family members or loved ones. As shared by Skinner, "Although tragic events are part of my nightly entourage, both professionalism and emotional survival require police officers to care from a distance. However, this suppression of feelings takes its toll at home and our personal relationships often suffer. I sometimes wonder if my family views me as a stranger—a living consequence of the stress" (Skinner, 1994).

This dynamic can make it difficult for the officer to deal with his or her own emotional struggles, or to be present and able to address difficulties being encountered by family members. Whether an officer, loved one or a distressed member of the community, the psychological pressure builds to a powerful crescendo. It is at this point that suicide may not only be considered, but may be seen as the most viable solution to the current situation.

GATEKEEPER TRAINING

Gatekeepers, or first finders, represent those people in every community or institution who, because of their contact with those at risk for suicide, are in a position to identify and refer people thinking about suicide or have already begun their journey to attempt suicide. The QPR gatekeeper-training module enhances general awareness about suicide, teaches the warning signs of suicidal thinking and behavior, and explains three basic intervention skills. The training module also includes a QPR information booklet and a three-part folding card, summarizing key information on the nature of depression and suicide, the role of alcohol in suicide crises, and, if necessary, how to access the involuntary civil commitment laws to save a life. At present, all 50 states have laws on the books to help interrupt the suicidal journey. Although these laws vary from state to state, when a law enforcement officer believes an individual may harm himself or herself, or commit suicide, the officer is obliged to contact a mental health provider to ensure that those individuals receive a mental health evaluation or take that person to a hospital.

Gatekeepers can be anyone trained in QPR. After QPR training of executives in a health maintenance organization, two women asked to speak privately with the instructor. The first woman stated, "A family friend told me my 16-year-old son held a pistol to his head at the Christmas party last week. Should I be concerned?" This question led to an affirmative answer and an immediate referral for evaluation of this teenage boy. The boy had been considering suicide for several weeks. Pointing a gun to his temple may have indicated a behavioral rehearsal.

The second woman told the instructor, "My husband has kept a revolver near our bed all of our married lives. He recently took it to the pawnshop and hocked it. When I asked him why he'd done that, he said 'Don't ask stupid questions!' What should I do?" In this case, the woman brought her husband to the instructor's office. The instructor, also a mental health provider, conducted a suicide risk assessment. Interestingly, the gentleman said, "I wasn't going to use the pistol . . . but I was going to go to the lake and gas myself."

In both of these cases, someone close to the suicidal individual, not a professional, asked the *question*, and the individual was *persuaded* to accept a *referral* for assistance. Such recognition and referral activity is common in the hours, days, and weeks after QPR training. Similarly, a mental healthcare organization found that, through mandatory QPR training for their staff, not only did they improve knowledge about suicidal risk factors and warning signs in their patients but also proceeded to conduct active interventions on several staff after the training occurred (LeBuffe, communication, 2000). It is very likely that lives were saved because of these interventions. That's what QPR is all about.

A REASON TO HOPE

By acknowledging and responding to the need to provide proper training, perhaps the nation's attitudes about suicide and prevention are changing. The oldest organization for suicide research and suicide prevention, the American Association of Suicidology, has aided and assisted a number of new organizations to grow and flourish. A group called Suicide Prevention Advocacy Network (SPAN) has been instrumental in advocating for suicide prevention and influencing the political system to recognize suicide as a national problem and to allocate funding to help in raising awareness and prevention activities. In recent years, other organizations have formed to further the cause of suicide prevention and to assist those left behind. These include the American Foundation for Suicide Prevention (AFSP), 1-800-SUICIDE, Suicide Awareness Voices of Education (SAVE) and Survivors of Law Enforcement Suicide (S.O.L.E.S.), and the National Police Suicide Foundation. Still other groups, such as the Law Enforcement Wellness Associates, strive to offer information and training to support law enforcement personnel on a variety of topics, including preventing suicide.

The Surgeon General of the United States has also been a leader in efforts to reduce the stigma associated with mental illness and has been a champion in suicide prevention, recently issuing his National Strategy for Suicide Prevention (Satcher, 2001). Suicide is being spoken about and changes are being made.

CONCLUSION

Although suicide is always complex, multidetermined, and multifaceted, most experts feel that most suicides can be prevented. Increased knowledge, coupled with straightforward intervention, can help cut through the denial, ignorance, resignation, and apathy many people feel about our ability to prevent suicide. Some people's cultural consciousness contains dangerous and erroneous myths about suicide, myths that add to the problem, not help solve it. Many of these societal myths serve to foster and reinforce the sense of hopelessness that suicidal people experience on their journey toward self-destruction. For example, if you believe suicide is inevitable and that it cannot be prevented, you are unlikely to act boldly when intercepting a suicidal communication. Likewise, if you believe that people who talk about suicide don't do it, you are unlikely to take a direct or indirect verbal suicide threat seriously. Sadder still is the case of one man who shared that he had been told that talking about suicide actually *lowers* the risk for suicide. Because of this misinformation, when a friend shared his plans to shoot himself, an opportunity for intervention was lost, and one more survivor of suicide was added to the population.

Suicidal people may communicate their intentions to commit suicide to several people or to only one other person. Therefore, everyone must learn what to do, but especially law enforcement support staff, dispatchers, administrative personnel, employee assistance providers, officers, family members, and community members.

These basic, necessary steps can be learned in as little as an hour and may save a life. If unable and/or unwilling to take such steps themselves, everyone must at least know who to contact if they become suspicious or concerned that someone they know may be considering suicide.

QPR does not require an advanced degree to administer, just as those applying CPR do not have to be physicians or cardiologists. In fact, assuming the role of diagnostician or trained counselor is discouraged. The act itself involves intervention and referral, not a formal psychological evaluation, ongoing treatment, or counseling. Merely learning what intervention steps to take, and when to take them, can mean the difference between life and death.

People expect an officer trained in CPR to apply knowledge and skill in an attempt to save the life of a citizen or fellow officer if they are not breathing and do not have a heartbeat. Wouldn't people expect the same officer, similarly trained in suicide prevention, to make a good-faith effort to save another life in peril? Indeed, a good faith effort to prevent suicide is not a matter of choice but a matter of duty.

REFERENCES

Anjeski, P. (Commander) (1996). U.S. Department of the Navy Suicide Prevention satellite training, September.

Baker, T. & Baker, J. (1996). Preventing police suicide. *FBI Law Enforcement Bulletin*, October, 24–27.

Field, G. & Jones, C. (1999). Code of silence doesn't help. *USA Today*, June.

Hill, K.O. & Clawson, M. (1988). The health hazards of street level bureaucracy: Mortality among the police. *Journal of Police Science*, 16: 243–248.

LeBuffe, P. (2000). Assistant Director with the Institute of Clinical Training and Research. Communication to the QPR Institute. Devereux Foundation. Villanova, PA.

McIntosh, J. (1998). Aggregated data supplies to the American Association of Suicidology and Indiana University of South Bend. National Center of Health Statistics.

National Center for Health Statistics. (1996). *American Association of Suicidology Public Information Sheet.*

Parker, T.J. (2000). *Red Light* (pp 216, 221–224). New York: Hyperion.

Sanders, G. (1999). Good Officers Gone Bad: PTSD Issues for Police Officers. *www.geocities.com/HotSprings/Spa/7762/sanders_01.html.*

Satcher, D. (2001). *www.mentalhealth.org/suicideprevention*

Skinner, B. (1994). Sacrificing normalcy: Police work is not just a job—it's a state of mind. *Police*, September, 94 & 91.

Violanti, J.M. (1995). The mystery within: Understanding police suicide. *FBI Law Enforcement Bulletin*, February , 19–23.

Violanti, J.M. (1996). *Police Suicide: Epidemic in Blue* (p 24). Springfield, IL: Charles C Thomas.

Violanti, J.M., Vena, J.E. & Marshall, J.R. (1996). Suicides, homicides, and accidental deaths: A comparative risk assessment of police officers and municipal workers. *American Journal of Industrial Medicine*, 30, 99–104.

Ward, N. (1997). *Clinical Aspects of Depression.* Paper presented at the "Workplace Strategies for Depression Conference." Portland, Oregon. January 10.

Chapter 5

DEPARTMENTAL BARRIERS TO MENTAL HEALTH TREATMENT: A PRECURSOR TO POLICE OFFICER SUICIDE

DICKSON DIAMOND

INTRODUCTION

After the death of a police officer by suicide, I am consistently asked the natural question one would ask of a psychiatrist: *"what would have caused a police officer to take his or her own life?"* By the time I've arrived on the scene, there has already been much speculation . . . "rumor has it that the officer had been under investigation for possible misconduct," . . . "I heard she had been recently dumped by her boyfriend,". . . "the officer had been having financial difficulties."

I must tell you, as I explain to police supervisors who have lost an officer to suicide, law enforcement officers do not commit suicide for the preceding reasons. In fact, the concept that situational events and life stressors are responsible for a police officer's suicide is just not true. What then is to explain a seemingly reasonable law enforcement officer's decision to resolve life's problems through such a devastating permanent solution? This takes me to the second most frequently asked question by management, "did their job as a police officer in any way contribute to the decision to end their life in this manner?" In other words, what management wants to know is whether those years working undercover, or having been involved in body recovery after the devastating World Trade Center tragedy, or having responded to one too many homicides involving children, contribute to this unforeseen act. I would hope this question is being asked not out of idle curiosity but to provide insight into the prevention of future officer suicides.

In answering this question one must understand that traumatic experiences, such as those endured by many law enforcement officers, no matter how horrific, do not cause an officer to commit suicide. Having said this, I believe that if officers who committed suicide had not chosen a law enforcement career, they would be alive today. This is not because they would have been spared the inherent traumas related to law enforcement work but because of other possible reasons to be made clear in this chapter.

THE ROLE OF DEPRESSION IN SUICIDE

The U. S. Surgeon General's Office recently released a report addressing the causes of suicide and strategies for its prevention. According to this report, a psychiatric condition, known as *"clinical depression"* is what's responsible for most suicides (The Surgeon General's call to Action to Prevent Suicide, 1999). This fact is something that psychiatrists have known for years. Clinical depression is a common disease, which affects 6.4 percent of the general population (Regier & Kaelber, 1995). Of this 6.4 percent, six percent will go on to commit suicide (American Association of Suicidology, 2001). There is no reason to expect that those in law enforcement possess any special immunity from this disease, or its sometimes fatal consequence. In other words, one would expect to see 6.4 percent of law enforcement officers with clinical depression, and an accompanying 6 percent of those officers going on to commit suicide.

As a manager, you might want to have some familiarity with a disease that affects such a high percentage of your fellow officers, especially when this disease is associated with a significant risk for suicide. Clinical depression is due to changes in concentrations of chemicals in the brain that regulate mood, energy, sleep, and appetite. It is not clear why some people develop this chemical imbalance, but it is clear that it has nothing to do with a weakness or a character flaw (a common misconception taken by many in law enforcement). The symptoms of clinical depression include a decrease in energy or increased fatigue and a loss of the ability to partake in enjoyable activities. With police officers, this often becomes evident, because it affects the routine workout in the gym. Sleep is also disrupted because of depression. People usually find themselves waking much earlier than usual, with difficulty falling back to sleep. A lack of sleep should eventually be spotted by management, as seen in an officer's physical appearance and lack of alertness. Concentration is also impaired by this disease. The combination of lack of sleep and impaired concentration typically results in poor requalifying scores on the shooting range, increased incidences of motor vehicle accidents involving the department vehicle, and poor work performance. As a component of this disease, one frequently becomes agitated, restless, and keeps to oneself. In addition, an officer's impulse control and ability to tolerate what was once considered minor irritations becomes impaired.

A good manager will recognize these symptoms, they are the tell tale clues that an officer has depression. A feeling of sadness, worry, and desperation tend to dominate ones thoughts. Officers with clinical depression must expend excess amounts of energy during work hours just to fight off these debilitating symptoms of depression and maintain a relatively competent level of functioning. When these symptoms persist longer than several weeks, the sheer exhaustion just to get through the day can result in significant consequences in an officer's performance at work and quality of life at home. Officers who have worked in particularly stressful environments or who have encountered significant traumatic situations on the job will experience an even greater impact. Alcohol has been the long accepted social activity of law enforcement officers off duty. It is not surprising to find officers who have depression increasing their intake of alcohol as a form of self-medication. Of course, this only serves to worsen already impaired concentration, impulse control, agitation, and intolerance for stress. Alcohol is a drug which itself causes the brain to become depressed when consumed frequently. It is not difficult to imagine how someone in this psychological state can make matters worse for themselves and their family, thus causing a classic downward spiral.

We have a natural tendency to search for reasons to explain why a person might have clinical depression. Remember that depression is caused by a chemical imbalance in the brain, most likely because of a genetic predisposition. Although job stress, drinking problems, marital discord, or financial or legal problems can affect this chemical imbalance, more often, it is the chemical imbalance that *precedes* these life stressors. The brain's thermostat, which regulates these chemicals, can malfunction without the help from outside stressors. In fact, as is the case with many medical disorders, even when in excellent physical and mental condition, depression can strike. Those who ask the question, *"I don't see why he should be depressed, he's got everything going for him,"* do not understand that depression, like other medical illnesses, just happens, unrelated to outside pressures or internal personal strength. When depression does hit, the disease interferes with our decision-making ability and tolerance for stress. The longer the brain's regulatory thermostat is allowed to malfunction, there becomes an increased likelihood that the individual's ability to cope on a day-to-day basis will become impaired. To the outside observer, the impaired actions and coping skills of the officer are all that is noticed, what remains hidden is the underlying cause of this impairment.

Many times, inappropriate conduct by an officer will come to the attention of internal affairs. It is only the astute investigator who recognizes that this officer's conduct is the result of an ongoing medical condition, clinical depression. Too often, by the time an officer is recognized as having depression, it is viewed as having stemmed from an ongoing internal affairs investigation, rather than the initial misconduct having stemmed from the effects of depression. I can think of several police suicides to which I have responded, where the first bit of information I am informed of is that the officer had been under investigation for some sort of misconduct. Assumptions are immediately made that the suicide was out of shame or guilt or that they just couldn't handle the pressure of the investigation. Perhaps in the movies these are reasons for suicide, but in real life, most suicides are a consequence of depression. When performing a psychological autopsy, looking for evidence that an officer had been having depression is critical. One can more easily understand an officer taking his own life, who had clinical depression than one whose life had been filled with stress but had no evidence of an underlying depressive illness. The chemical imbalance in the brain results in such feelings of internal pain and hopelessness, so that when accompanied by impairment in judgment, decision making, and impulse control, suicide is seen as an attractive option.

TREATMENT FOR DEPRESSION

Nowadays, treatment for clinical depression is readily available. TV commercials depicting cartoon characters urge us to ask our doctor about Prozac® or Zoloft®. These medications are as frequently prescribed as those for acid indigestion and high blood pressure. What makes these antidepressant medications so popular is that they work so well. Within three weeks of taking these medications, the symptoms of depression begin to disappear. What this means to the depressed law enforcement officer is restored full nights of sleep, energy returning to normal levels, and a resumption in partaking in enjoyable activities. Also dramatically improved is an officer's concentration, impulse control, and outlook on life.

Commonly, law enforcement officers take the "macho" approach, preferring to "tough it out" without medication, attempting to overcome this disease on their own. It is important for them to understand that these medications do not mask the symptoms of depression, they actually correct the chemical imbalance responsible for the depression. Of course, talking a law enforcement officer into getting treatment for depression requires a bit of a selling job. Officers typically have concern about the potential for addiction and side effects. I reassure my patients that these particular medications (antidepressants) are not addicting and have very few side effects. They are nontoxic, which is good news to the psychiatrist who is prescribing the medication to patients, who may potentially have suicidal thoughts.

Other concerns expressed by those in law enforcement include a fear of being turned into a "zombie" and a loss of the ability to experience feelings. I believe much of those concerns, as well as a resistance to taking antidepressants by law enforcement officers, stems from their strong need to be in control. They fear that this little pill may have the ability to take that control away. I reassure them that they will gain a feeling of increased control over their life as a result of the medication, rather than any loss of control.

What about those "brave" officers who are willing to tough it out? These are the officers who I am very concerned about. According to the Surgeon General's recent report, untreated depression is the number one risk factor for suicide. In other words, antidepressant medication can save lives. As a psychiatrist, I must also stress the added benefit of therapy, along with medication. I have had mixed experiences with the types of psychotherapies law enforcement officers tend to receive. Many officers who do seek psychotherapy gravitate to unconventional forms of treatment, believing this to be an appropriate alternative to medication. Police officers with symptoms of depression are first encouraged to be evaluated by a psychiatrist to determine whether antidepressants are indicated. It is useful to have the psychiatrist make additional treatment recommendations that complement medication, such as the type of psychotherapy best suited for the officer's condition. Many health care plans encourage initial assessment and treatment of depression by a general practice physician, rather than a psychiatrist, as this is more cost-effective. I discourage this practice, because it oftentimes results in the officer receiving inadequate treatment for his or her depression and a lack of the necessary ongoing medication follow-up visits.

Clinical depression is common in the general population and, like high blood pressure and diabetes, it is not surprising that a fair number of law enforcement officers will have it. As with high blood pressure and diabetes, many people are medically predisposed to develop clinical depression. This predisposition to depression has nothing to do with being weak, and it has little to do with a career in law enforcement. If the risk of developing depression is not associated with law enforcement work, and we know that depression is a precursor to suicide, how does one explain the fact that members of law enforcement have a risk of suicide three times greater than the general population? Does law enforcement select for people who have a greater predisposition for depression, or is there something about a career in law enforcement that causes those officers who do have depression to be more likely to commit suicide then those in the general population who have the same illness?

Let's go back to those members of your force who have high blood pressure or diabetes. Are they receiving medical treatment for these conditions? Of course they are. We know that left untreated, both these disorders can lead to stroke, heart attack, and other medical complications. Now let's suppose that your department had a policy requiring officers who receive treatment for high blood pressure, to report this. Furthermore, it was common knowledge within your Department that many of these officers are placed on administrative after following reporting their treatment.

Imagine one of your officers learns that he has high blood pressure during a routine physical. He is reassured by his physician that as long as he remains on medication, he will be fine. This officer, fearing the possibility of being placed on Department administrative leave, chooses to go against medical advise and not take the prescribed medication. Ten years later, after a foot pursuit of a perpetrator, he has a major heart attack and dies. One might ask what role your department played in his death, and might a change in department policy have had a role in its prevention? This officer had a controllable medical condition, which did not have to go on to cause heart disease. Had this officer felt free to treat his blood pressure, heart disease would not have developed, and the physical challenges of the job would not have resulted in his death.

Modern medicine has decreased the risk of dreadful complications of diabetes and high blood pressure developing. Modern law enforcement has increased the risk of suicide among its own officers by discouraging the treatment of mental health disorders, such as depression, which can lead to suicide. In fact, police officers are much more likely to die from a self-inflicted gunshot wound than one delivered by an adversary. Although it would certainly be politically incorrect for a law enforcement agency to come right out and say that we discourage our officers from receiving medical treatment for depression, the message is clear . . . *"if you are being treated for depression, be prepared to surrender your weapon, forget any chance of an elite assignment such as undercover or SWAT, and you can kiss any hope of making a higher grade goodbye."*

There are police officers who live in fear, hiding a deep dark secret . . . that they have depression, and even worse . . . that they are receiving treatment for this medical condition. I frequently receive unanimous calls as a police psychiatrist from officers inquiring , *"If I am on Prozac, will my gun be taken away from me?"*, *"Will my supervisor be told that I am taking an antidepressant?"* *"Is my career over if I continue on Paxil?"* Then there are the calls from the supervisors, *"I just found out one of my officers assigned SWAT is on Prozac, what should I do?"* *"I've got an undercover officer who we believe is on Zoloft, how should we handle this?"* The message management is sending to its employees is clear, "we've got a problem if we discover that you are getting treatment for depression." Recently, an officer described to me his experience with hearing loss resulting from years spent on the firing range. He had been told by physicians that a hearing aid would dramatically improve this deficit. Fearing that a hearing aid would be a dead give-away to management of his medical condition, he chose to struggle through his career with this impairment. One does not have to look too far to see the irony of this situation.

POLICE DEPARTMENTAL POLICY AND TREATMENT

When department policy, whether perceived or true, prevents its officers from receiving adequate treatment for a medical condition, there is a problem. This is a problem that can be corrected by good management. But first, it is crucial to understand that when someone has clinical depression, it not only causes a depressed mood, it also affects ones ability to concentrate, impairs judgment, and slows down one's reaction time. As one well aware of the physical and emotional requirements to be fit for duty as a law enforcement officer, of course I would have concerns for an officer on active duty who has from clinical depression. There is a major distinction here between the officer who takes medication to keep depression under control and those that live day to day with untreated depression. The goal for management should be to encourage treatment, not to encourage denial of the illness. Although I receive many calls from supervisors concerned about officers who they discover are receiving treatment for depression, it is the rare occurrence that I receive a call with concerns over an officer who exhibits symptoms of clinical depression in the workplace and is not getting medical treatment. The concern by management is on the wrong medical issue. It is not the officer receiving treatment that I'm concerned about, it's the one who isn't that is of concern. By changing this emphasis, management can create a healthier police force and a decrease in the incidence of suicide among its officers.

This remains a challenge because of the culture of law enforcement. If an officer is taking antidepressant medication prescribed by a psychiatrist, there is no escaping the label, *"I suffer from depression."* It is this label that seems to be the kiss of death within law enforcement. To avoid such a label, and the stigma that goes along with it, many in law enforcement believe that they must avoid treatment. It is treatment that raises the red flag to management that a problem exists. Police officers, who in the past did opt for treatment, spent much time devising ways to get around the reporting system required during their yearly physical. During this physical, officers were asked to declare all current medications being taken and any mental health treatment. By discontinuing antidepressant medication the day before the physical, some believed they could state in good conscience that they currently were not receiving psychiatric treatment. It is a shame that one feels he or she must hide the fact that appropriate treatment for a medical condition is being taken.

Attempts to obtain relief from the painful symptoms of depression, while avoiding the detection and stigma of this illness, have resulted in some officers seeking relief by taking self-prescribed remedies, such as herbs, or allowing noncredentialed therapists to provide unconventional treatments. Others have sought relief of their symptoms by taking antianxiety medications or sleep medications, which they obtain from their family physician. These types of medications can be addicting and do have potential side effects that can interfere with an officer's ability to perform his or her duties safely. Although these medications do not treat depression, like alcohol they serve to temporarily mask the symptoms of depression. These unfortunate practices have led to several police officer suicides in the past, because they allow depression to go untreated. I believe that law enforcement agencies want to do the right thing for their officers, however, attempts to correct this perception by having policies that state, "each incident will be handled on a case-by-case basis," do nothing to ease officers' concerns when deciding whether to seek treatment for their illness.

We must now consider the practical side of this problem from a management point of view. Can we have officers on the street enforcing the law while taking these medications. Certainly, this is a very different story than if they were employees of a noncritical occupation. These officers carry guns, testify in court, and sometimes maintain Top Secret security clearance entrusted with National Security matters. Although management's concerns tend to focus on the medication, I believe that the real issue remains, "I've got an officer with a psychological weakness." This way of looking at a medical condition only reinforces the officers' perception to avoid treatment, and thus avoid being labeled as emotionally defective. One must keep in mind that there is a big difference between an untreated illness and one that is being treated and controlled with medication.

During a visit to a agency facility after a female police suicide, I was approached by an officer who was informed by his partner that he was taking Prozac for depression. This officer voiced concerns to me, stating, *"there is no way I'm having anyone back me up whose on Prozac."* It was difficult for me to conceal my frustration at his ignorance. I replied, *"so you would prefer your backup to be suffering from untreated depression, self-medicating his symptoms with alcohol!"*

Back to management's concerns about medication. The simple fact is that none of the medications used to treat depression have any side effects that would impair an officer's ability to perform his or her duties. Actually, these medications enhance concentration and judgment while restoring physical energy and an emotional sense of well-being.

The only likely side effect people taking these medications experience is an inability to have an orgasm. To date, I have not found this to be a problem for police officers in carrying out their routine duties.

When concerns are raised by upper level management regarding medication side effects, I routinely state that I am much more concerned about the side effects caused by high blood pressure medication. High blood pressure medications do have the potential to interfere with certain physical and emotional tasks. I say this knowing that many in upper level management are taking these blood pressure–lowering drugs. Another common concern raised by management regarding medication is the fear that an officer known by management to be taking one of these antidepressants may become involved in a shooting incident, in which, a civilian is accidentally wounded or killed. Can knowledge by management of this officer's treatment come back to haunt them? The answer is that management has the practice of good medicine on their side. One cannot attribute a bad shoot to the officer having been on an antidepressant medication, nor can one attribute a bad shoot to an officer having a diagnosis of depression, so long as that officer's treatment is medically appropriate, and the symptoms of depression are currently controlled by the medication. What would be considered negligent on behalf of management is the officer who has depression but has avoided seeking appropriate psychiatric treatment because of perceived department policies and its negative repercussions.

Let's return to the Surgeon General's report, which is a call to action to prevent suicide. In this report, it is clear that untreated depression is a major risk factor for suicide. One can reduce the risk of suicide in a police department by increasing the likelihood that those officers who have depression obtain appropriate medical treatment. This can only be achieved by removing existing department policies that serve as barriers to mental health intervention. According to the Surgeon General's report, having barriers to mental health treatment is yet another major risk factor for suicide. A department's barriers to mental health treatment may not be written on paper but solely perceived to exist by its officers. Unfortunately, the end result remains the same, officers do not feel free to seek mental health treatment without facing possible repercussions. To diminish this perception, departments may need to create new policies clearly describing its approach to officers receiving treatment for mental health conditions. A Police Department's Employee Assistance Program can do little to encourage officers to obtain treatment for depression, when department policy sends a different message.

One last suicide risk factor identified in the Surgeon General's report pertains to all law enforcement officers. Individuals who have easy access to weapons have been determined to be at an increased risk for suicide. Several years ago, after conducting a psychological autopsy of an officer who committed suicide, I was asked by the supervisor whether I thought she would be alive today had she chosen a different profession. Most individuals who do contemplate suicide don't readily have the means at their disposal to successfully complete the job. Being depressed, they also may not have the energy or motivation required to obtain these means. Many suicide attempts are unsuccessful because of ambivalence or the use of nonlethal means in an attempt to get the job done. A police officer's easy access to and familiarity with their weapon makes an impulsive, poorly thought-out suicide attempt a permanent reality.

Unfortunately, I have been called on too many times to determine the cause of an officer's suicide. Looking back, I can't help but recognize the presence of these three risk factors in each case. Depression is a common medical disorder that can be found in people of all works of life. Although easy access to a weapon is an inherent part of a career in law enforcement, easy access to mental health treatment should be as well.

REFERENCES

American Association of Suicidology. (2001). *Facts sheet: Suicide and depression;* www. suicidology.org

Regier, D. & Kaelber, C. (1995). Epidemiology catchment area program In Tsuang, M., Tohen, M. & Zahner, G.E.P. (Eds.), *Textbook in Psychiatric Epidemiology.* New York: Wiley.

U.S. Public Health Service. (1999). *The Surgeon General's Call to Action to Prevent Suicide.* Washington, DC: USGPO.

Chapter 6

SUICIDE AND THE POLICE CULTURE

JOHN M. VIOLANTI

INTRODUCTION

Recent evidence suggests that there is an elevated risk of suicide within law enforcement. Violanti, Vena, and Marshall (1996) found that police officers had a suicide rate eight times that of police homicide and three times that of work accidents. Compared with male municipal workers, male police officers had a 53 percent increased risk of suicide over homicide, a threefold rate of suicide over accidents, and a 2 ½-fold rate of suicide over homicide and accidents combined. Guralnick (1963) found the suicide ratio of male police to be approximately two times that of the U.S. male population. Suicides accounted for 14 percent of police deaths compared with 3 percent of deaths in all other occupations, and more officers died as a result of suicide than homicide.

Violanti (1996) examined data from five police departments in the United States and found most police officers who committed suicide were Caucasian men, of lower rank, used a firearm, and had alcohol involvement. New York City Police data indicated that 77 percent of police officers who committed suicide were less than 35 years of age, and 73 percent had less than 10 years of police service. Fifty-seven percent of these suicides were believed to be precipitated by relationship difficulties (Ivanoff, 1994). A study of Royal Canadian Mounted Police suicides found officers to be of lower rank and in police service for an average of 11 years. Suicides were precipitated by psychological difficulties, relationship problems, alcohol abuse, and other life strains (Loo, 1986).

THE POLICE CULTURE AND SUICIDE

Entry into law enforcement involves a process of abrupt change from citizen to police officer. The rookie officer's adaptation of a new work role occurs interactively at individual and social levels (Harris, 1973). The process of change from civilian to police officer is very strong in basic police training and continues to dominate officers' lives throughout their career.

Just ask any police officer, and they will tell you that "police work gets in your blood. You become it and it becomes you." Socialization into the police role begins early in police training, which attempts to instill a sense of superhuman emotional strength in officers (Violanti, 1996). From the very first day in the police academy, recruit officers are told that they are someone unique, far different from the average citizen, and certainly beyond harm. During training, police recruits are further reinforced with skills of self-defense, "talking people down," street survival techniques, and extended firearms use. In addition, they are well armed and protected with bulletproof vests. By the time recruits leave the academy, they are strongly ingrained into the police role.

To the average young person coming into police work, the job may at first seem exciting and adventurous. Officers can become addicted to such excitement and become part of what Gilmartin (1986) calls the "brotherhood of biochemistry," a physiological, as well as social, dependency on the excitement of police work. Gilmartin suggested that police work leads officers to alter the way they deal with the rest of the world. Officers quickly adapt to excitement and danger and become psychologically depressed in calm or normal periods. Police officers often become listless and detached from anything unrelated to police work. At home they feel uneasy and have difficulty adjusting to the role of spouse, father, or friend. Some officers begin to treat their family like suspects on the street, unable to separate police work from their personal life.

Van der Kolk (1987) found that persons like police officers who are involved in highly stressful jobs may actually become addicted to excitement and danger. The increased arousal brought about by dangerous or exciting events decreases the individual's ability to assess the nature of current challenges and interferes with rational decision processes.

Given this research, it seems that police officers, through psychological and physiological mechanisms, become ingrained in police work and isolated from other life roles such as family, friendships, or community involvement. Subsequent psychological depression and social isolation may result.

Becoming a Cop: Formal and Informal Culture

Many forces mold persons into the role of police officer. The formal and informal police work culture may exert considerable influence on the individual in this regard. The police organization may be said to strongly demand individual adherence to the police role (Whisenand, 1989). Police behavior is constrained and shaped by others in the system: judicial decisions, legislation, the media, and special interest groups. Common in police structures are military-style rank positions, specific work roles, and impersonal work relationships. The police organization is unique from others because of the *intensity* with which it restricts officers into their work role—intensity resulting from rather powerful combinations of militaristic and bureaucratic control methods (Violanti, 1996). Officers are coerced to behave consistent with the police role in a continuously changing environment and punished when they do not conform (Gross, 1973).

Such actions of the police organization may lead to stress in officers. First, the police organization restricts officers into rigid behavior patterns that diminish the ability of officers to assume other roles (Kirschman, 1983). Second, the organization places the officer on the defensive by what Kirschman described as "deflection of blame"–a form of bureaucratic control that protects the reputation of the organization at the expense of its members. Third, the police organization not only prescribes specific roles but also dictates how officers must fulfill these roles. One result is what Harris (1973) called "false personalization," a facade of behavior that forces officers to act out roles that are contrary to their true identities and feelings. Officers who use false personalization may fail to attend to their true psychological self. They forsake themselves and other role identities for those prescribed by the police organization.

The informal police culture also places pressure on officers to conform. This close-knit culture prescribes a theme of solidarity among officers, which seems to help them deal with rejection from the greater society (Neiderhoffer, 1967). The foremost requirements are loyalty (i.e., an officer never "rats" on another officer) and a prescribed code of secrecy.

How Does the Police Culture Affect Officers?

Being ingrained in the police role can reduce one's ability to deal with stress inside and outside of police work. Reasoning, social, and inflexible styles associated with the police role hinder effective coping with stress and heighten risk factors associated with the potential for suicide.

Officers ingrained into the police culture take on an array of preconceived ideas and behaviors that become a permanent part of their personality (Bonafacio, 1991; Skolnick, 1972). Police officers tend to view reality as a "black and white," and are often inflexible in their thinking. Officer's view of themselves as problem solvers precludes the luxury of searching for meaning in work events. This spills over into their personal lives and problems (Stratton, 1980).

Dealing with problems from the perspective of police work constricts thinking to "all-or-nothing." This sort of thinking can cause problems when officers are faced with complex life difficulties. Shneidman (1986) noted that such thinking may increase the risk for suicide:

> Synonyms for constriction are a tunneling or focusing or narrowing of the range of options usually available to that individual's consciousness when the mind is not panicked into dichotomous thinking: either some specific total solution or nothing . . . one of the most dangerous aspects of a suicidal state is the presence of constriction . . . the penchant toward dichotomous thinking is commonly seen in the suicidal person.

Shneidman adds that good adjustment involves being able to view frustrating life situations from many angles rather than simply black and white. Adjustment to stress lies in the individual's ability to make discriminations along the "black and white" line. Those capable of making such distinctions are less likely to choose a solution of suicide. When faced with chronic stress, officers socialized into the police role may decide to cope with this same sort of thinking. The potential for suicide may increase as officers attempt to deal with stress from an all-or-nothing perspective.

Adherence to the police role not only limits thinking abilities but also the use of other social roles for reduced stress. Thoits (1986) argued that the *more* social identities a person has, the *less* potential that person will have for depression or psychological stress. In the case of officers ingrained in the police culture, "culture identity" is very much restricted to police work, putting them at a serious disadvantage for coping with stress.

Thus, as a consequence of the police culture, officers may deal with most life situations, good or bad, from the standpoint of their police role. This raises the question of the impact of the police role on life relationships that may precipitate psychological stress—personal, police peer, and societal relationships.

The Police Culture, Relationships, and Suicide

Previous research has indicated that problems with interpersonal relationships may increase the potential for suicide. Robin's (1981) account of the detailed case histories of 134 suicides, for example, is filled with accounts of difficulties in interpersonal relationships before the final suicidal act. Conroy and Smith (1983) reported that 18 of 19 suicide cases involved a significant family loss, such as estrangement from family members, death of significant others, or divorce or separation issues between spouses.

Personal Relationships

Police officers seem to have problems with relationships. Ivanoff (1994) found that relationships were a primary factor in 58 percent of police suicides in New York City over the past ten years. Officers were involved in extramarital affairs, were recently separated or divorced, or had conflict with supervisors at work. One reason for relational difficulties may be an emotional detachment from others. The role of a police officer calls for *depersonalization*—interpersonal relationships, on the other hand, call for *personalization* (Violanti, 1996). The police culture socializes officers into *not* expressing emotion, to put up an emotional barrier to protect themselves from the human misery they witness. When officers are off-duty, however, they cannot turn their emotions back on. They remain stuck in prescribed "tough guy" roles that are seen as necessary to be an effective police officer (Madamba, 1986). As a result, the personal relationships of police officers are not *personal* at all; they are more like transactions on the street. Significant others soon become less important to the police officer. Compassion is subdued in favor of the police culture, which takes precedent over most other emotional feelings. In some respects, the police role becomes a safe place to hide but at the same time does not allow for an outlet of emotions. The inability for police officers to use other roles to solve problems with a family person, friend, or lover may be behind many police relationship problems. Below is an example of a relationship problem that ended in suicide:

> Two weeks before his death in mid April, This officer, 26 years old, told friends he wanted to kill himself. He felt caught, he said, between two women. He was deeply involved with one but planning to become engaged to the second. He had been on the force four years. A colleague of the dead officer spoke of stress on the job. "Unfortunately," he said, "the department does not teach how to deal with it well. It's a big organization and some people get lost."

Bonafacio's (1991) data from New York City found that the police department provided assistance to officers who had relationship problems but focused on *changing others* and not the officer. The department tried to impress on spouses or friends that police work is difficult and that they should be supportive of officers. To the department, the police role was seen as unchangeable and others outside the role must adjust.

Police Peer Relationships

Dependence on the police role may affect relationships with peers. Loyalty and cohesiveness are important expectations of the police role, and those who violate the unwritten code of police brotherhood may pay the price of rejection by the group (Brown, 1981). To degrade or bring shame on the police becomes a moral trespass and may increase the potential for what Durkheim (1952) termed "altruistic" suicide. The military is another example, where the individual has no clear sense of a distinctive existence and is ready to sacrifice the self for the group (Campbell, 1981). In such a situation officers may view themselves as counting little; and interest is subordinated to the police group which is seen as paramount.

Some police suicides may be therefore be based on shame or inability to fulfill role expectations of the organization, police peers, the public, or oneself. Following is a case of police suicide that involved perceptions of bringing dishonor to the role of police officer:

> This suicide involved an officer who was thirty years old and a recent graduate of the police academy. Two days after graduating from the Police Academy and a day after being assigned to a Precinct, the officer became intoxicated, and struck another car, slightly injuring two people. Instead of stopping, he sped off and later reported his car stolen. New officers are on probation for their first two years and the charges would have been enough to end the officer's career. He apparently shot himself in the chest with a handgun in his basement apartment amid empty beer cans. Nearby was a display of his uniform and his equipment set up in such a way that one official described it as "a shrine to the police department." He left a note apologizing to his parents and the department for any disgrace he might have brought them.

Police peers likely contribute to feelings of shame and guilt. Statements found in police suicide notes like "I let the guys down" confirm the need of officers to fulfill their police identity. The potential for suicide may be the result of a perceived unforgivable offense against the police role and the job.

Relationships with Society

Police relationships with society at large are also affected by police culture identity. Police officers, because of the nature of their job, may become isolated from family, friends, and general society (Stratton, 1984). Experience in police work leads officers to perceive an uneasy relationship between society and themselves; society is anyone who is not a police officer—they are perceived as the "enemy," and the police are the protectors of justice. Thus, police officers in their culture purposely isolate themselves from society. Most social activities revolve around police organizations, and only other officers are considered true friends (Niederhoffer, 1967). Durkheim (1952) argued that isolation is an important factor in suicide. His research demonstrated that isolated individuals or groups were more likely to commit suicide.

DISCUSSION

This chapter has posited that the police culture restricts flexibility in thinking about the world from other than the police view and the use of other life roles in dealing with stress. In sum, these factors impair the police officer's ability to deal with psychological stress. As a result, the potential for suicide may increase.

It should be made clear that one cannot blame suicide completely on the police culture. Culture may be but one of many circumstances that increase the potential for suicide. Suicide is a complex phenomenon that involves the interaction of many risk factors. In a study of lifetime variables in persons between the ages of 15 and 85 years, factors such as gender, age, race, personality, life experiences, prior socialization, and psychological disposition all contributed in varying degrees to completed suicide (Vaillant & Blumenthal, 1990).

Certainly the police recruit selection process can be an important tool in reducing the incidence of psychological problems and perhaps suicide among police officers. It is interesting that as of 1990, 51 percent of police agencies in the United States did not use psychological screening in their recruit officer selection process (Strawbridge & Strawbridge, 1990). It may also be beneficial to test police officers after entrance at various times throughout their career. Researchers have found that officers with several years on the job reported more somatic symptoms, anxiety, and alcohol vulnerability. These were considered important precipitants to depression and suicide in police officers (Hyatt & Hargrave, 1988).

Suicide prevention should be an important goal for police organizations. At present, there seems to be a lack of suicide awareness training for police officers and care for survivors of police suicide (Sawyer, 1996). One suggestion might be to include training on suicide prevention in stress management programs. A second suggestion might include an organizational restructuring of the importance of the police role. New officers should be made aware that the role of police officer is important, but that it is not the only role in their lives. Recruits might be encouraged through sensitivity training to actively participate in family activities and establish friendships outside of policing. The narrow view of the police as "friend" and every else as "foe" should be strongly discouraged. With the advent of community policing in America, the police now have a great opportunity to enforce the law by working with the community in many roles (Manning, 1989).

It is considerably difficult to disentangle the complex causal web of police work and suicide, however, one point remains clear: far more research into every aspect of police suicide is necessary. Such an effort is crucial if police work is to become an occupation in which individuals can work with satisfaction and psychological health.

REFERENCES

Blau, T. H. (1994). *Psychological Services for Law Enforcement.* New York: Wiley.

Bonafacio, P. (1991). *The Psychological Effects of Police Work.* New York: Plenum (pp. 169–174).

Brown, M.K. (1981). *Working the Street: Police Discretion and the Dilemmas of Reform.* New York: Russell Sage.

Campbell, T. (1981). *Seven Theories of Human Society.* New York: Oxford University Press.

Conroy, R.W., & Smith, K. (1983). Family loss and hospital suicide. *Suicide and Life-Threatening Behavior,* 13, 179–194.

Dash, J., & Reiser, M. (1978). Suicide among police in urban law enforcement agencies. *Journal of Police Science and Administration,* 6, 18–21.

Durkheim, E. (1952). *Suicide.* Glencoe, IL: Free Press.

Freud, S. (1954). *The Origins of Psychoanalysis.* New York: Basic Books.

Gilmartin, K.M. (1986). Hypervigilance: a learned perceptual set and its consequences on police stress, In J.T. Reese & H. A. Goldstein (Eds), *Psychological Services for Law Enforcement.* Washington, DC: US Government Printing Office. (pp. 443-446).

Gross, E. (1973). Work, organization, and stress. In S. Levine & N.A. Scotch (Eds), *Social Stress* Chicago: Aldine Publishing (pp. 54–110.)

Guralnick, L. (1963). Mortality by occupation and cause of death among men 20-64 years of age. *Vital Statistics Special Reports,* Vol. 53. Bethesda, MD: Dept. of Health, Education and Welfare.

Harris, R.N. (1973). *The Police Academy: An Inside View.* New York: Wiley (pp. 45–78).

Hyatt, D., & Hargrave, G. (1988). MMPI profiles of problem police officers. *Journal of Personality Assessment,* 52, 722–731.

Ivanoff, A. (1994). The New York City police suicide training project (pp. 5–15). New York: The Police Foundation.

Kirschman, E. (1983). *Wounded heroes: a case study and systems analysis of job-related stress and emotional dysfunction in three police officers.* Doctoral Dissertation. Ann Arbor, MI: University Microfilms International..

Lester, D. (1992). Suicide in police officers: a survey of nations. *Police Studies,* V. 15, 146–148.

Loo, R. (1986). Suicide among police in a federal force. *Suicide and Life-Threatening Behavior*, V. 16, 379–388.

Madamba, H.J. (1986). The relationship between stress and marital relationships in police officers. In J.T. Reese & H. A. Goldstein (Eds), *Psychological Services for Law Enforcement*. Washington, DC: US Government Printing Office (pp. 463–466).

Manning, P.K. (1989). Community policing. In R.G. Dunham & G.P. Alpert (Eds.), *Critical Issues in Policing*. Prospect Heights, IL: Waveland (pp. 395–405).

Niederhoffer, A. (1967). *Behind the Shield*. Garden City, NJ: Doubleday.

Reiser, M. (1974). Some organizational stressors on police officers. *Journal of Police Science and Administration*, V. 2, 156–159.

Robins, E. (1981). *The Final Months: A Study of the Lives of 134 Persons Who Committed Suicide*. New York: Oxford University Press.

Sawyer, S. (1996). Police Suicide and Survivors. Presentation at National Conference of Concerns of Police Survivors (COPS), Las Vegas, Nevada, January 13.

Shneidman, E.S. (1986). *Definition of Suicide*. New York: Wiley (pp. 121–147).

Skolnick, J. (1972). A sketch of the policeman's working personality. In G.F, Cole (Ed.), *Criminal Justice: Law and Politics*. California: Wadsworth (pp. 20–42).

Stratton, J. (1984). *Police Passages*. Manhattan Beach, CA: Glennon Publishing.

Strawbridge, P., & Strawbridge, D. (1990). *A Networking Guide to Recruitment, Selection, and Probationary Training in Major Police Departments in the United States*. New York: John Jay College.

Thoits, P.A. (1986). Multiple identities: examining gender and marital differences in distress. *American Sociological Review*, V. 51, 259–272.

Vaillant, G.E., & Blumenthal, S.J. (1990). Suicide over the life cycle: risk factors and span-life development. In S.J. Blumenthal, & D.J. Kupfer (Eds.), *Suicide Over the Life Cycle*. Washington, DC: American Psychiatric Press (pp. 1–17).

Van Der Kolk, B.A. (1987). *Psychological Trauma*. Washington, DC: American Psychiatric Press.

Violanti, J.M., Vena, J.E. & Marshall, J.R. (1996). Suicide, homicides, and accidental death: a comparative risk assessment of police officers and municipal workers. *American Journal of Industrial Medicine*, V. 30, 99–104.

Violanti, J.M. (1996). *Police Suicide: Epidemic in Blue*. Springfield, IL: Charles C Thomas (pp. 10–86).

Violanti, J.M., Vena, J.E. & Marshall, J.R. (1986). Disease risk and mortality among police officers. *Journal of Police Science and Administration*, V. 14, 17–23.

Whisenand, P. (1989). Personnel selection. In W.G. Bailey, (Ed), *The Encyclopedia of Police Science*. New York: Garland.

Chapter 7

TRUST AND THE SUICIDAL POLICE OFFICER

CLAUDIA L. GREENE

EARLY CLUES

An experienced police officer often has a sense that something is amiss in the neighborhood that he patrols on a regular basis, because "something does not feel quite right." His usual pattern of psychosensory experience of the scene is disrupted in some indescribable way. Similarly, the experienced officer may feel that "something" has changed in his interaction with the fellow officer who is losing (or who has lost) his ability to trust.

When an officer begins to lose trust, the early clues may not be verbal ones. Instead, the first thing you may notice is that the officer begins to pull away during interpersonal interchanges in barely perceptible physical ways. His stance, interpersonal distance, and eye contact may be altered slightly. His partner or training officer, who routinely and closely observes his interactions with citizens in the field, may be the first to notice the change. This slight distancing may then spread to the officer's interactions with his partner or the FTO.

The officer's interpersonal behaviors may also change. He may not be as easy going, or he may be more rigid than usual. His sense of humor may be restrained or may reflect his underlying fear or rage (usually the latter). He may not laugh at jokes, clown around, or participate in practical jokes that he once enjoyed with his partners. He may not "be fun to be around" any more and have lost his social

76

enjoyment. He may seem preoccupied and quiet or more irritable. He may suddenly become irritable, when in the past he was placid and relatively unflappable. He may start taking shortcuts with safety procedures and the letter of the law. He may become more lax in dealing with some citizens and more rigid in dealing with others. He may be the subject of citizen complaints about the use of excessive force, disrespectful conduct, harassment, or discrimination. Fellow officers may wish that he would "lighten up." At home, his spouse, significant other, children, family, and friends may feel that something is wrong but not be able to put their finger on the problem. They just know that something is "not quite right." Children complain that Dad has "changed." His rigidity on the street may infiltrate his behavior and interpersonal interactions at home. His children may complain that he has become a tyrant or that he does not care about them anymore. He may become controlling to a humorous degree (threatening to handcuff the young man who dares to ask his daughter out on a date, and then riding shotgun in the patrol car while chauffeuring them). Or, he may become so paranoid that he refuses to let his children become involved in age-appropriate social activities for fear they may come to some bad end.

THE SHIELD GOES UP

As people start to notice the nontrusting officer pulling away in interpersonal interactions, they begin to mention their observations and ask questions. They express their concern and may ask him repeatedly what is wrong. The more they want to help, the less trusting the officer becomes. A vicious circle begins. The harder his loved ones and colleagues knock at the door and ask to be let in, the more nails the officer puts in the door. The officer gradually builds a (sometimes not so) silent barrier between himself and the ones concerned about him and his lack of trust. The more his loved ones and friends attempt to communicate their feelings and concern, the more he hides his own feelings. The closer his loved ones and friends want to be, the farther away he wants to be, and the more he maneuvers consciously and unconsciously to push them away. The same dynamic occurs with his police partner, who in many ways is even closer than a spouse or significant other. The people trying to help the officer describe him as interpersonally "icy," "cold," "uncaring," or "withdrawn." The shield has "gone up." In many cases, it is impenetrable, even by mental health professionals.

LATE STAGES

This progressive loss of trust rarely occurs in isolation. By the time mood, anxiety, psychotic, or personality disorder symptoms or substance abuse emerge, the loss of trust is usually far advanced. Like an infant in the absence of the nurturing support and safety of a constant and consistent caregiver, the officer fears that he can trust no one but himself with his physical and emotional survival. He feels alone, isolated, abandoned, and impotent. He is enraged that his demands are no longer met and that no matter what he does, his demands are ignored. Because he now gets his sense of self-worth from his ability to control others, he is soon disillusioned about his own sense of personal competence. He is humiliated about his loss of control and his great feeling of vulnerability. He fears annihilation, just as does the helpless infant, although in his position of authority, his culture does not allow him to feel helpless or express helpless feelings. He has been taught that he is invincible on the street, yet he cannot even control his own trust. Depression, panic, general anxiety, substance use, and even loss of reality testing follow. In each of these states, he has to find a release for his rage. It can be directed toward himself, as self-mutilation, substance abuse, or suicidal ideation, or toward others, as assault, homicide, or combined homicide-suicide. His impulsivity and poor judgment, free access to firearms, and expertise in their use increase the hazard.

WARNING SIGNS OF IMMINENT ACTION

By the time the nontrusting police officer reaches the point that he is considering suicide, he has lost all sense of trust in himself, in his meaning and abilities, in his hopes and dreams, in his family and friends, in his spiritual source or power, and in his past, present, and future. He has lost the glue of human experience. Without trust, he can no longer form meaningful attachments to other people. His significant relationships are heavily tarnished. No longer does each person remain individual. The officer clings tightly to his loved ones subconsciously, so as not to lose them; but in actual behavior, he pushes them away to protect himself from their potential abandonment. He can no longer share deeply with his loved ones, or form reversible attachments to them. Separations, both physical and emotional, are painful; part of him "dissolves" when the other party leaves. Painful and terrifying feelings of annihilation overwhelm him. He feels utterly alone. He can rely on no one, not even himself. He sees no way of escape. Suicide is his only choice.

Only at this late date does the mistrusting officer begin sending overt messages about his suicidal ideas and intent. He may visit his family doctor with various nonspecific physical complaints. He may make contact with friends and acquaintances to say "goodbye" in idle chat. He may try to give away prized possessions. He may slip death references into his conversations or make morbid jokes. He may draft suicide notes and formulate hard plans to end his life. He may suddenly clean his gun, after neglecting this duty for awhile. He may caress it, sleep with it, go to a gun store or show and look at higher power models. He may get out his old ballistics manuals or go to the range at odd hours to practice. He may be unusually competitive or intense at the range. He may buy different types of ammunition, load and unload the magazine repeatedly, cradle the bullets in his hands, inhale their scent, and imagine "eating" his gun. He may try a "dry run" of the act, holding his unloaded gun to his temple or put it in his mouth. He may play Russian roulette with an empty gun. He may plan his death scene, Having death scene investigation experience, he may plan his final scene to be pristine or gory, depending on whether he wants a "kind" or "angry" goodbye. He may go through the motions to "get it right." He may sit in the bath tub and plan angles of trajectory and towel location to minimize blood spatter. He may try out a noose with a loose knot. He may write out meticulous timetables for his remaining hours, or he may write out his own death scene investigative report. He may hoard his medication for overdose, if he is taking psychiatric medication or medication for medical problems. He may size up his family medicine chest for potentially lethal medications. He may research the lethal dosages of medication. He may borrow or even steal medication from friends and family members. He may fondle knives in the kitchen, sharpen them, and check their sharpness by shaving a bit of hair off of his arm. He may place the cold steel blade flat against his throat or wrist. With further resolve, he may place the blade against his skin and press to the point that he inflicts a tiny laceration. He may empty a bottle full of pills into his hand and contemplate them. He may make preliminary, planned, nonlethal cuts or gunshots, or swallow sublethal doses of pills. He may leave suicide notes in conspicuous spots, or call a friend or emergency services immediately after preliminary, superficial attempts to harm himself. He may call a friend to rescue him. He may set up the time and place of the scene to ensure that he will be found before he dies and to increase his chances of rescue. Sometimes these calculated plans, which reflect the ambivalence of his decision to die, backfire and he dies accidentally.

The situation is different when the officer cannot trust at all. He may weigh the differing degrees of lethality and efficacies of his considered suicide methods. He may decide to use a highly lethal chemical, high-power firearm, massive overdose, prolonged exposure to poison gas, or a disguised accident to commit suicide. He may set the scene in such a remote area that there is no hope of rescue. He may not be found until his remains have been skeletonized. Or he may express his rage flagrantly and commit suicide at his substation, in his patrol car, or at home, in front of those he wants to punish. Just as the physical violence of police domestic disputes reflects only the tip of a long-smoldering psychological volcano, so the final physical acts just before suicide reflect long-smoldering rage, loss of trust, fear, humiliation, shame, abandonment, betrayal, and other negative core emotions.

Once the suicidal officer performs these ritualistic final acts, some of the pressure of the final decision subsides. He may suddenly show signs of great relief and improvement of his mood, as if a major problem has been solved. He may become truly cheerful and astonish family, friends, and colleagues by his sudden change in demeanor. His energy level may suddenly increase. He is in mortal danger. He has made the decision to die. He is at peace with himself and his decision. The problem of how to stop the pain has been solved. Death is imminent.

IMPACT OF TRUST PROBLEMS IN THE SUICIDAL POLICE OFFICER

Spouse, Significant Other, and Family

Trust is the glue of social relationships. If there is no trust, there can be no true interpersonal attachment. Trust is also required for intimate relationships, in which each party retains his identity and does not merge or fuse with the other, overwhelming him. If a relationship initially founded in trust is suddenly or gradually subjected to the loss of trust by one of its partners, the other partner feels the uncertainty as a barely perceptible change in the quality of their bond. As the lack of trust increases in one partner, the bond begins to quiver in an off-key way, transmitting its distress to the other partner, who also then begins to doubt and lose trust. A vicious circle begins, because suspicion and even paranoia become "contagious." Away from the job, the spouse, significant other, or children will likely be the first to notice the change in the quality of the interpersonal bond. It will then spread rapidly throughout his relationships with the rest of his family and friends.

The Police Partner

The partner is closer in many ways to the officer than the spouse or significant other. Partners eat, breathe, and communicate "on the same wavelength," because they learn to think alike in the field. They may even develop similar physical mannerisms and walk and talk alike. Motorcycle patrol officers who have ridden together for years move as a single unit and interact flawlessly and fluidly in a dance. As in a long-term marriage, police partners may finish each other's sentences and know what the other is thinking without a word being said. These abilities come from long hours spent together in the mundane tasks of the street, as well as in the foxholes of survival there. Trust is essential for physical and psychological survival of the officer pair on the street. Trust is the only thing that allows one officer to lay down his life for another. The bond between police partners is even more sensitive to barely perceptible changes in levels of trust than that between the officer and his spouse. Accordingly, the police partner often feels the loss of trust even before the officer's loved ones and family.

Fellow Police Officers

Fellow officers must be able to trust that they will cover each other in life-threatening situations. Without this trust, officers cannot do their jobs. If there is no trust between officers, all the energy normally used in watching the street and responding to the needs of its citizens must be diverted to watchfulness to remain alive. The police officer is taught to monitor the mental state of others, whether "bad guys," informants, or citizens on the street. He is always listening and evaluating what is said, how it is said, what is not said, body language, and how the other person makes him feel inside. He is always monitoring his personal radar about the relative level of safety (physical and psychological) between other people and himself and others. His monitoring eventually extends to his co-workers, although it may be at a subconscious level. Just as a stone thrown in a pool of water causes ripples to expand ever outward, the lack of trust in one officer can touch many others. This effect can occur in one of two ways. The individual officer can interact with many of his fellows, who directly experience tension in previously formed professional and/or personal bonds. Or the partner can transmit the change in the troubled officer by transferring the increased tension of their bond to his interaction with others. The co-workers may notice the subtle change in the officer's or partner's personal interactions, overhear snatches of their conversation, experience a change in the quality or developmental level of their humor, or observe a change in the quality or efficiency of the job product of the officer or the partnership. The co-workers will likely have questions.

Police officers are often good armchair psychologists. They make and share observations and conjectures and discuss them privately among themselves. The more striking their observations, the more intense their interest. The greater the conjecture, the wider the range of discussants. The troubled officer loses his privacy. Civilian employees overhear "things." Soon rumors begin to fly. They are eventually heard by the officer and his partner. The officer's suspicions escalate, he questions his partner's loyalty, and tempers flare. The stress on the partnership is visible to all, and more vicious circles begin. Many cracks and splits appear among the officers: officer vs. partner, partnership vs. co-workers, partner vs. co-workers (when the partner defends and protects the nontrusting officer), officer vs. co-workers, and co-workers vs. co-workers (as other officers "take sides"), etc. The mistrust of co-workers and rumor may be taken home to affect police wives and children. These parties will then interact in a different way with the officer's significant other, spouse, and children, creating further suspicion and another vicious circle.

Police Squad of Assignment

Specialty squads usually deal with high-risk situations, such as violent crime, narcotics trafficking, gang violence, barricade situations, and child endangerment. Trust plays a critical role in the cohesion of these squads. One of the best examples is the trust required between a tactical team and its sniper. The sniper may be far from the command post and fellow tactical officers. However, he must be trusted to supply critical intelligence, to kill swiftly, and to bring a situation to a safe conclusion for the others involved. If there is no trust, there can be no team cohesion, because there can be no true attachment between team members. With trust, very strong bonds form between team members. One will take a bullet for one another, because the bond is so strong. Just as with partners, team members who are well meshed anticipate each others thoughts, develop private language and rituals, move physically in similar ways, share a common humor, and know instinctively what each others needs are. They are a string of highly polished, mobile, individual spheres on a vanadium steel wire. They move and twist together and withstand any external force together. Trust is the vanadium in the steel wire. It gives the wire its strength. If one officer begins to lose trust, it is as if a tiny knot develops in the wire. The team cannot twist and turn smoothly. As the officer loses more trust, more and more knots appear. Soon the team is a tangled mess, with the initial officer not trusting his team mates, the team mates not trusting him, and the team mates splitting among themselves. Lines are drawn between those who support and those who do not support the initial, nontrusting officer. Soon the team unravels. The humor level drops, and the nature of the humor changes. Camaraderie deteriorates into in-fighting. Cliques form. Trust is lost between cliques. The cliques and team members avoid one another, subtly or not so subtly. This avoidance can lead to shortcuts and tactical errors in the field. Officers can die as the result of one officer's inability to trust. The team disintegrates.

Police Substation

Whereas the specialty team can be likened to spheres on a vanadium wire, each subgroup in the station house is equivalent to a row of beads on a thread. The substation can be likened to a woven fabric formed of interwoven police and civilian strands. The fabric of a healthy substation is tightly woven, much like Kevlar, so that it can resist large outside stresses and assaults. Like Kevlar, however, it is not fortified against penetrating (ice pick) or cutting (knife) injuries. These sorts of instruments can slide through the gaps between the interwoven fibers or slice right through them. Trust is the stabilizer of the substation's Kevlar-like fabric. It binds the warp and weft strands together, strengthening the interpersonal interactions of large numbers of officers and civilians working different shifts and bringing cohesion and unit identity. Substations have different personalities. These personalities are in large part related to the degrees of trust existing between groups and individuals at various levels of their organization-command to troops, troops to command, troops to each other, one rank to the next, police to civilians, civilians to police, men to women, and old hands to the inexperienced, and vice versa, and between individuals of various ethnic, religious, and philosophical backgrounds. If there is trust in the station house, the warp and weft threads will come together to give each bead (individual) a place in a uniform weave. A strong smooth fabric results. If one or more people at the substation cannot trust, the smooth weave is interrupted. Knots appear along with holes. Some parts of the fabric unravel. The Kevlar-like sheet is now a moth-hole-ridden piece of poorly knit material. The holes between the interwoven threads are so big that any sort of external threat or assault can enter the station and cause inestimable damage, all because of the virus of distrust.

If a substation's personnel are grounded in trust, and its fabric is strong, the introduction of a nontrusting officer can still cause problems. That one individual spreads the virus of mistrust to the partnership, then co-workers, then teams, and then to the station house. The infection may be subtle. It may not flare until a challenge by an outside force suddenly shows that the Kevlar-qualities of the station house fabric have melted quietly away. The virus of mistrust is so tiny that it slips easily through the Kevlar-like weave of the substation fabric, just like an ice pick. Associated rumors slice through the fabric of trust, just like a knife. Such conditions may be the catalyst for a nontrusting officer's final decision to end his life. When he does, the partnership, fellow officers, specialty teams, and the substation fall with him. Just as no man is an island, police officer suicide is not an isolated phenomenon.

Police Department

As a whole, the department is greater than the sum of its parts. Its men, partnerships, teams, and substations can be likened to a symphony, with a myriad of instruments providing different parts of the melody. For a coherent result, the different instruments and sections must intermesh seamlessly. The same is true for a police department. Once again, trust is the glue that keeps the melody coherent and on key. The department can also be likened to a patchwork quilt composed of pieces of fabric (substations) of different weaves. We have seen how the lack of trust can act as a virus and spread from one officer to affect an entire substation. The holes in its fabric (created by the lack of trust) affect the entire quilt. The holes spread as the virus of mistrust spreads. Because officers and civilian personnel transfer back and forth between substations, the virus of mistrust spreads easily. Rumors help spread the mistrust. They are carried by officers and civilians traveling between station houses in the usual course of business, at break times, and after hours, when police socialize with their own. Police chat rooms on the Internet are a particularly powerful venue for these rumors. They allow rapid transmission of mistrust, the lack of trust, and paranoia.

The Public

To a police officer and his department, there are two "publics." One is composed of the citizens he serves and enforces ("good guys" and "bad guys"). The other consists of the citizens in authority (city hall or other governmental bodies that oversee the function of both the department and the individual officer.) Trust (or lack of it) markedly influences the interaction between the officer and both of his "publics." Much of the trust is historical. Do the citizens and governing body support its police officers? Appropriate respect, salaries, benefits, living and working conditions, and concern for family and psychological well-being all show support of the police department. Up-to-date training, the latest equipment, and standing behind the officer when he performs his duty appropriately, but is caught up in a sensational media feeding frenzy, are all indicators of trust in its officers. What is the citizen and government response when the officer injures or kills someone (suspect, convicted fugitive, civilian) in the line of duty? How do the citizens and government respond when an officer is injured in the line of duty? How helpful are the workman's compensation benefit plan and support services for the officer and his family? How much public support is there for the family when an officer is killed in the line of duty? Is the same response given to a family whose officer was fatally shot by a "bad guy" as one killed on a freeway working a traffic fatality? What is the public response to an officer with a fatal illness? In general, the degree of public support of its police officers determines a great deal of the trust that the department and its officers have in the public. The degree of public trust in its police officers is directly related to the degree of trust shown by the officer to his citizens and governing body. Citizen responses that engender trust reap benefits. Officers will likely return that trust when there is the possibility of a benefit of a doubt. However, the issue of trust can be hazy. The command staff has to trust city hall, because it is the lifeline for the funding of the department. Close liaisons may develop between the highest levels of command and city fathers. Gradually, in the eyes of the line officer, the Chief and his immediate staff become part of city hall. If the Chief does not support his troops (on pay issues, investigations, benefits, top notch equipment, attention to the general quality of life on the Job for the rank and file, and the like). He will be equated with "one of them" and will not be trusted. This breech of trust will soon spread quickly from the bottom of the organization to the top. In response, the Chief and command staff may lose trust in the rank and file. The virus of mistrust then spreads rapidly from the top of the organization down. Splits occur between the command staff, now "allied" with City Hall, and the officers in the trenches. It becomes an "us" versus "them" situation. Everyone loses, especially the citizens. Politics rapidly rears its ugly head, as citizens line up with whichever side benefits their own interests the most. Real police work, in which officers have pride in their profession, their

Department, and their city, comes to a halt. A passion for helping turns into a job. Cynicism runs high, troop morale sinks, rank and file turn against rank and file, gender turns against gender, ethnic background turns against ethnic background, the young turn against the experienced, substation turns against substation, and colleague turns against colleague. Officers begin to cut corners under stress. Mistakes are made, because officers focus on other issues, not on the mission proclaimed at academy graduation. It becomes every man for himself. Officers quit. Officers act out their frustrations. Harsh words are exchanged. Retaliatory transfers, demotions, and internal affairs investigations occur. Union and collective bargaining issues and more politics come to the fore. The divide between command staff and the rank and file deepens further. Officers become despondent. Substance abuse (especially of alcohol) rises. Depression and anxiety rise individually, as well as collectively. The lack of trust spreads from individuals to groups. It soon becomes generalized at an institutional level. Officers feel the loss of control. They may become more aggressive on the street, because they feel procedures are changed to give citizens ("bad guys") the benefit of the doubt. Charges of abuse of power or even police brutality may arise, as officers attempt to regain psychological and physical control of the streets. The department begins to disintegrate internally, with decreased efficiency and productivity, less service to the public, and, in the long term, a possible increase in crime. "When the cat's away, the mice will play." As departmental morale crashes, individual officers struggling with the lack of trust and associated depression lose their scaffolding of job constancy and consistency, as well as their ability to trust their own. This may be the final straw. Departmental chaos based on lack of trust can send the officer struggling with lack of trust into a tailspin. If associated with depression, anxiety, and substance use, it is a fertile ground for suicidal ideation, and even suicide.

Chapter 8

EFFECTIVE POSTVENTION FOR POLICE SUICIDE

Robert Loo

Schneidman (1981) coined the term "postvention," in contrast to prevention, to describe the sorts of actions taken after a suicide largely to help survivors such as family, friends, and co-workers. Postvention was seen as a natural extension to the established suicide prevention field partly because there will always be some base level of suicide even when highly effective suicide prevention programs exist and partly because the survivors of a suicide can be viewed as victims of posttraumatic stress (i.e., posttraumatic stress disorder: PTSD) and, therefore, in need of assistance in dealing with their grief reaction.

SURVIVOR REACTIONS TO POLICE SUICIDE

The signs and symptoms of distress and bereavement resulting from the suicide of an officer might be a mix of any of the following commonly reported reactions among survivors (DSM-IV, 1994):

- Shock over the suicide;
- Feelings of grief;
- Feelings of helplessness;
- Feelings of abandonment, isolation, and loneliness;
- Feelings of depression and weepiness;
- Feelings of guilt because they believe that they might have been able to prevent the suicide;

- Sexual dysfunction;
- Suicidal thoughts . . . the contagion effect;
- Anger towards the suicided, the police department, other survivors, or the media;
- A loss of interest in work, family and friends, and other activities;
- Increased work absences, lateness, and use of sick leave;
- Alcohol and drug abuse; and
- Disruptive sleep and eating patterns.

STEPS IN SUICIDE POSTVENTION

The major steps in postventions could include any or all of the following depending upon the circumstances.

- Establish and execute your standing operating procedure (SOP) for postvention. The SOP should specify the key positions/persons responsible for initiating the SOP. For example, the immediate supervisor, the officer who first hears about the suicide (e.g., the duty officer), the departmental psychologist/health professional, padre/clergy, and internal affairs.
- Have a crisis team trained and ready to have a planning meeting to initiate the critical incident stress debriefing (CISD). The team could be a mix of health professionals and trained peer counselors.
- Notify the departmental administration, next-of-kin, family physician, and clergy if known, and other key persons.
- A departmental communication release should be made as soon as is practical to let fellow officers and staff know the facts rather than have the grapevine circulate rumors. Manage the external media by having a timely press releases, so that facts rather than rumors reach the media.
- Have a carefully picked debriefing facility readily available. Although it may be practical to use a room in a police facility, an off-site facility such as a meeting or conference room in a community health center might be better for the survivors.
- Do at least one follow-up session to address unresolved concerns and any new issues that arose since the debriefing.
- Conduct a confidential evaluation of the postvention by hav-

ing participants complete, for example, a confidential and anonymous evaluation questionnaire a week or two after the debriefing to identify particularly what worked well and what needs to be improved for future postventions. Alternatively, the evaluation might be conducted as a group session, thus allowing for interactions among survivors but precluding anonymity.

ETHICAL ISSUES AND DILEMMAS

The issue of suicide contagion is important, because police are armed and can readily commit suicide in an impulsive but undo-able moment. Police supervisors and health professionals must be alert to any warning signs (e.g., verbalizations about committing suicide, mood changes such as becoming despondent) that a survivor himself or herself is experiencing suicidal ideation or intent. Such persons must be referred to a qualified health professional in suicide prevention.

A MODEL FOR SUICIDE POSTVENTION

Figure 8.1 presents a model for suicide postvention for police,

Figure 8.1
Model for Suicide Postvention

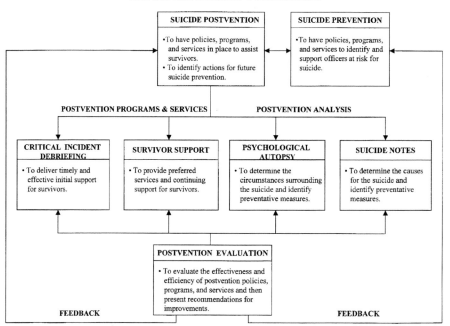

which the remainder of this chapter follows. As seen in the model, two program areas are emphasized, the critical incident debriefing and survivor support, and two analysis actions, the psychological autopsy and the analysis of suicide notes. As seen in the figure, all components of postvention must be evaluated, particularly for their effectiveness, and improvements should be made for the future. Finally, the linkage between prevention and postvention is highlighted.

CISD

The CISD, originally developed to help emergency services personnel such as police and firefighters to cope with traumatic incidents, can be used to help survivors too. The CISD usually has the following characteristics:

- CISD typically uses a single session, a half-day or even full-day session, although survivors may be referred to health service providers, clergy, or other sources for additional assistance if required.
- CISD usually uses a group session (10–12 survivors) partly so the various survivors have the opportunity to share their common grief and provide mutual support and partly for efficiency, given the likely limited number of experienced health services professionals readily available for this purpose. The group session can be seen as a "decompression" session in an emotionally safe and supportive setting for survivors.
- CISD should occur within one to three days of the suicide, so support can be provided in a timely manner to ameliorate the distress of survivors.
- A secluded and safe location is used to provide privacy and confidentiality.
- The selection, training, and experience of a facilitator or group leader is critical to ensure that the CISD process is conducted effectively. The facilitator should be a health services professional with extensive training and experience in CISD, PTSD, suicidology, and the grieving process (Farberow, 1992). It can be helpful to have a survivor act as co-leader if a survivor has the personal characteristics (e.g., emotionally stable, empa-

thetic, effective interpersonal communications skills) and leadership qualities (e.g., can keep the group focused) to facilitate
the process.

Steps in Critical Incident Debriefing

The following steps are typically found in CISD (e.g., Mitchell &
Dyregrov, 1993).

- The facilitator describes the process and sets the ground rules
  for the session, particularly the need for confidentiality and a
  mutually supportive environment. The introduction of participants.
- Participants need to express their feelings about the suicide
  and the perceived reasons for the suicide. The results of such
  sharing in a safe and supportive group session should be emotional decompression and sense-making about the suicide.
- The facilitator or group leader should be able to use the group
  discussion to draw out the multitude of signs and symptoms of
  distress, as well as the grieving process for the group, to examine and then move on to the important actions that help manage distress and grieving. Such actions could include continuing to meet as a self-help group to continue providing one
  another with support, linking to community services, conducting a stress self-assessment, techniques to improve open communication about suicide among family members and significant others, and performing deep muscle relaxation exercises
  to overcome muscle tension and aid sleep.
- An after action report should be prepared and disseminated to
  the police department and health professionals, not simply as
  an administrative procedure but as a means of sharing points
  learned and pitfalls to avoid in future CISDs.

SOCIAL SUPPORTS FOR SURVIVORS

Conservative estimates report that there may be as many as 28
persons directly affected by a suicide (Knieper, 1999). One could
argue that, for police suicides, the number of significant survivors
could be much higher given that not only family and friends are

directly affected but virtually all of the police officers in a department, especially small departments where strong bonds create a family feeling. Clearly, there is a need to provide support for these many survivors. Research has shown that survivors report receiving less support than desired or report being unaware of what support was available to them (e.g., Wagner & Calhoun, 1991). Such findings indicate that organizations need to do a better job of identifying survivors and communicating to them the availability of support services. For police departments, the imperative is to provide support for the family and fellow officers.

One potential issue is the macho image that still persists among some officers, that is, it is seen as a sign of weakness to ask for help or to actively participate in sessions for survivors. Another potential issue is the stigma associated with suicide in contrast to death by other causes such as vehicle accidents. For example, research found that widows of suicide tend to experience rejection from their husband's family and friends (Saunders, 1981). The point is that some survivors might be less likely to seek assistance or discuss the event with others, because it was a suicide. Police departments might consider a policy requiring that officers attend CISDs and other activities intended for their assistance to ensure that all affected survivors receive at least some assistance.

Although social support services initially brings survivors together for group and/or individual sessions, survivors may wish to form or to join existing survivor groups (visit the American Association of Suicidology at *www.suicidology.org* to see an extensive listing of survivor groups across the United States).

THE PSYCHOLOGICAL AUTOPSY

The term "psychological autopsy" and the practice of performing psychological autopsies grew from the frustrations experienced in the Los Angeles County Chief Medical Examiner Coroner's Office in the late 1950s where some deaths could not be properly resolved based on the collected evidence (Schneidman, 1981). By changing to a multidisciplinary approach, the Death Investigation Team, involving behavioral scientists in addition to the traditional medical experts, greater success resulted in (psychological) autopsies. In addition, interviewing informants such as family members, friends, family physician, and co-workers added much independent information about the suicided and circumstances (Brent, 1989).

Since that time, the term and process has evolved and broadened in scope; we are concerned only about the psychological autopsy in the context of police suicide. For us, psychological autopsies are useful in addressing three broad questions.

What Was the Mode of Suicide?

Because most police who suicide use their service handgun, the method of suicide is usually easy to confirm. In some cases, such as hanging, asphixiation (e.g., carbon monoxide poisoning from vehicle exhaust), or drug overdose, the mode of suicide can also be easily confirmed. On the other hand, some cases can be more difficult to resolve, because they involve multiple methods; for example, a drug overdose and drowning in a bathtub. Even more difficult to resolve are suicides that may appear as accidental deaths. For example, the single-vehicle fatal accident in which an officer drives at high speed into a solid barrier, when there are no mechanical, road, or weather conditions that can be proposed as reasonable explanations for the apparent accident.

There are several main reasons for gathering these data. The obvious reason is to identify use of the service handgun or other departmental weapon such as a shotgun so that access might be better controlled, hopefully, to make future suicides using departmental firearms more difficult.

What Were the Circumstances Surrounding the Suicide?

Determining when and where suicides occur might have implications for prevention (Lester, 1997).

- Did the suicide occur on or off duty?
- Did the suicide occur on a weekday, weekend, or holiday?
- Did the suicide occur at night or during the day?
- Did the suicide occur at home, a police facility, patrol vehicle, or other notable location?
- Did the suicide occur on an anniversary or other special day?

- Did the officer give away personal effects just before the suicide or make other gestures suggesting a "farewell" "a settling of accounts," or reconciliation with others?
- Was there a noticeable mood change before the suicide?
- Was alcohol or drugs a factor at the time of suicide?

These data could identify patterns suggesting periods when managers and helpers need to be especially vigilant about potential suicides so that preventive actions could be taken. For example, if mood changes precede suicide, then supervisors and officers should be trained to identify such changes to help identify high-risk officers.

Why Did the Officer Commit Suicide?

This is a critical question, not only for identifying preventive actions but it is a question raised by survivors who might benefit, in a small way, from having the answer. Family, friends, and fellow officers raise this question wondering what could have been so disturbing in the officer's life that suicide was the way out. For many officers suicide follows not just a single problem or critical event but the culmination of several overwhelming problems such as combined marital problems and career frustrations.

Ethical Issues

In conducting a psychological autopsy, one must treat all information and documentation as confidential. The integrity of the deceased must be respected. One must be careful not to cause further distress to survivors, for example, in the interview process. It is preferable that health professionals who are governed by a code of ethical conduct and subjected to disciplinary action by their professional body conduct interviews of survivors and informants. In any case all members of the team conducting the psychological autopsy need to be selected for their related expertise and personal suitability.

SUICIDE NOTES

A substantial percentage of those who suicide leave suicide notes;

a variety of studies over the past few decades showed that 15 to 35 percent leave notes (e.g., Shneidman, 1981; Tuckman, Kleiner, & Lavell, 1959). The analyses of suicide notes yields many insights into the factors that led to suicide, the person's state of mind, and other important factors. For example, Brevard, Lester, and Yang (1990) identified nine themes from 20 notes from a city in Arizona. The most important themes included the desire to escape from pain (12 of 20 or 60 percent of notes) and self-blame for events (13 of 20 notes or 65 percent). Leenaars (1991), who has worked extensively in this area, identified eight patterns in suicide notes.

- Unbearable psychological pain and suicide as the escape from such unbearable pain.
- Problems in establishing and maintaining interpersonal relationships.
- Rejection-aggression, that is, the turning inward of aggression rather against another person.
- The inability to adjust and overcome personal difficulties, or the perceived inability to adjust.
- The suicide note may serve as an expression of conflicting or ambivalent feelings about suicide, such as wanting to be dead but also wanting to be rescued and to live.
- Identification-egression in that the person has an intense attachment to a lost or rejecting person. If this emotional need is not met, then suicide might be seen as the only solution.
- Ego, that is, the suicidal person himself or herself is viewed as a cause of the problem if the person is unable to overcome their personal difficulties and wishes to die.
- Cognitive constriction, that is, rigid, impoverished, and concrete thinking, possibly as one result of trauma, might contribute to a person's decision to commit suicide.

Some researchers have focused on alcoholism because of the strong association between alcohol abuse and suicide or attempted suicide. For example, Leenaars and Lester (1999) found in their analyses of 16 notes from alcoholics a suggestion that suicide is associated with a response to unbearable pain, often associated with alcoholism itself; and a history of trauma such as a failing marriage. Thus, suicide may be seen as an escape from an unbearable situation.

Other researchers compared suicide notes written by men and women to detect gender differences, but these studies usually report no gender differences in themes (e.g., Canetto & Lester, 1999; Leenars, 1988; Lester & Heim, 1992). Age has been examined to determine whether there are any differences in themes between younger and older persons who commit suicide. Lester and Reeve (1982) found that older persons tended to be more concerned about feelings rather than actions and less explicit about their intended suicidal action. More recently, Leenaars (1992) found that older persons tended to write more about painful personal problems, about being trapped by despair, and long-term instability, for example, alcoholism or the multiple loss of significant others. To these findings is added the more obvious difficulty that some older persons, especially in our youth-oriented culture, can experience in adjusting to the vicissitudes of aging with its accompanying decline in physical functioning and health (Bauer, Leenaars, Berman, Jobes, Dixon, & Bibb, 1997).

EVALUATION OF POSTVENTION

Policies and programs for postvention must be evaluated periodically just as policies and programs in other areas such as crime prevention and community policing need to be periodically evaluated or audited. Evaluations help management, as well as other stakeholders (e.g., the community):

- Identify areas for improvement;
- Give recognition for a job well done;
- Assess the cost/benefit of the services provided, as well as potential opportunities for cost savings (e.g., outsource particular services), especially because police departments operate under limited resources;
- Assess the ethical and legal aspects of the policies and programs for critical incidents or areas for improvement to protect users of postvention and the department from litigation; and
- Assess the fit between postvention policies and programs with the department's other personnel and operational polices and programs.

Such evaluations should address at least the following questions regarding policy and programs (Patton, 1980, 1986).

Policy Area

Relying on an informal, unwritten policy or procedure, perhaps based on past departmental practices, might not be a prudent approach, given the scrutiny police services face and the potentially harmful effects of critical media coverage among other potential effects.

- Does the department have a written policy(ies) addressing postvention? If not, why not?
- How does the policy(ies) compare with those in other police departments and organizations?
- Have situations arisen that the policy does not address? If so, then identify required revisions to the policy(ies).

Program Area

Policies are simply sterile paper policies unless specific programs, services, and procedures are implemented to genuinely take action on desired policies. But it is also appreciated that program implementation and management is much easier said than done, especially when resources are tight or there is resistance to programs.

- Do the programs and services comply with the policy(ies)? If not, does the policy(ies) require revision or do programs and services need to be revised?
- What do the programs and services cost? Are the costs justified? Are there more cost-efficient ways of delivering the programs and services?
- Are the programs and services having beneficial effects for the stakeholders? Are there any unintentional negative effects on stakeholders?
- How do the programs and services compare with postvention programs and services in other police departments and organizations?

Resourcing

Resources are scarce in police departments, and the priority for resources understandably goes to the needs of operational policing before support services such as postvention. That said, managers and other stakeholders need to be creative in resourcing postvention, for example, can health and other professionals be co-opted to provided some services pro bono, or could community facilities be used gratis during no-demand periods for group meetings?

- Are the programs and services adequately staffed?
- Are qualified professionals managing the programs and services?
- Are the facilities, equipment, and other resources adequate?

Stakeholder Satisfaction

There are many different stakeholders in postvention, and it may be impossible to satisfy the divergent, or even conflicting, wants of the different groups. However, we must make a reasonable effort to satisfy stakeholders.

- Are the various stakeholders (e.g., survivors, departmental managers, police officers, local legislators and community leaders, health and community service providers) satisfied with postvention? What are their perceptions of postvention?
- What improvements can be reasonably made to better satisfy the stakeholders?
- Does the policy(ies) and programs neglect any stakeholder group?

Ethical and Legal Compliance

It is recognized that codes of conduct or legislation can be in conflict and that such issues need to be resolved.

- Is there full compliance with ethical codes covering, for example, confidentiality of medical and service files?
- Is there full compliance with departmental policies, regulations, and administrative procedures?

- Is there full compliance with legislation at the local, state, and federal levels?

Evaluation Issues

Although periodic evaluation makes good sense, not all departmental managers and stakeholders would likely embrace evaluations for a variety reasons.

- Departmental managers and supervisors might resist an evaluation for fear of being criticized or because they believe that the evaluation process would be too disruptive to the program.
- Some stakeholders might see an evaluation as a waste of resources in terms of staff and an evaluation budget, especially if there have been no serious criticisms or critical incidents.
- Some might wonder if the evaluation will be objective or simply a management tool for self-promotion or some hidden agenda.
- Some might believe that any recommendations will not be activated and that the evaluation will have little impact on postvention.
- Some stakeholders might be fearful that evaluators and others will get access to confidential or sensitive documents.
- A potentially serious problem is that required data and information to address the evaluation questions are not collected and available to the evaluation team. The need to have a confidential and secure data-capturing and reporting system is necessary at the start of programs.

The Evaluation Team

Particular attention has to be paid to the composition and credibility of the evaluation team. The team should have representation from departmental officers and the police union, qualified health professionals, survivors, and community stakeholders without becoming so large as to be unwieldy. The mandate of the evaluation team and reporting structure must be clearly defined, perhaps adopting existing guidelines used for audits or other program evaluations. The team must be on guard so as not to become co-opted by one or another stakeholder group but remain objective and "professional" in their work.

The Evaluation Report

To be useful, the evaluation report must:

- Present a balanced assessment showing good findings and areas for improvement
- Identify the limitations to the report, for example, areas in which data were not available
- Present specific, practical recommendations, preferably with the outline of an action plan
- Maintain the confidentiality and anonymity of contributors
- Be distributed or, at least, available to the stakeholders

CLOSING COMMENTS

Although postvention cannot bring back those officers lost to suicide, we should be able to provide timely and effective support to survivors and learn valuable lessons that will help minimize the likelihood of future police suicides. Review the model for suicide postvention in Figure 1 to ensure that police departments do cover the major postvention areas as discussed in this chapter and improve postvention for the future.

REFERENCES

Critical Incident Stress Debriefing

American Psychiatric Association. (1994). *Diagnostic and Statistical Manual of Mental Disorders* (4th ed: DSM-IV). Washington, DC: The Association.

Farberow, N.L. (1992). The Los Angeles survivors-after-suicide program. *Crisis, 13* (1), 23–34.

Mitchell, J.T. & Dyregrov, A. (1993). Traumatic stress in disaster workers and emergency personnel. In J. P. Wilson & B. Raphael (Eds.), *International Handbook of Traumatic Stress Syndromes*. New York: Plenum Press.

Williams, T. (1993). Trauma in the workplace. Ibid.

Postvention

Shneidman, E.S. (1981). Postvention: The care of the bereaved. In E. S. Shneidman, *Suicide: Thoughts and Reflections*, 1960–1980 (pp. 157–167). New York: Human Sciences Press.

Cain, A.C., & Shneidman, E.S. (Eds.). (1972). *Survivors of Suicide*. Springfield, IL: Charles C Thomas.

Psychological Autopsy

Beskow, J., Runeson, B., & Asgard, U. (1990). Psychological autopsies: Methods and ethics. *Suicide and Life-Threatening Behavior*, 20(4), 307–323.

Brent, D.A. (1989). The psychological autopsy: Methodological considerations for the study of adolescent suicide. *Suicide and Life-Threatening Behavior*, 19(1), 43–57.

Lester, D. (1997). *Making Sense of Suicide: An In-depth Look at Why People Kill Themselves*. Philadelphia: The Charles Press.

Shneidman, E.S. (1981). The psychological autopsy. *Suicide and Life-Threatening Behavior*, 11(4), 325–340.

Shneidman, E.S., Farberow, N.L., & Litman, R.E. (1970). *The Psychology of Suicide*. New York: Science House.

Social Supports for Survivors

Cain, A.C., & Shneidman, E.S. (Eds.) (1972). *Survivors of Suicide*. Springfield, IL: Charles C Thomas.

Knieper, A.J. (1999). The survivor's grief and recovery. *Suicide and Life-Threatening Behavior*, 29(4), 353–364.

Saunders, J.M. (1981). A process of bereavement resolution: Uncoupled identity. *Western Journal of Nursing Research*, 3, 319–335.

Wagner, K., & Calhoun, L. (1991). Perceptions of social support by suicide survivors and their social networks. *Omega, 24*, 61–73.

Suicide Notes

Bauer, M.N., Leenaars, A., Berman, A.L., Jobes, D.A., Dixon, J.F., & Bibb, J.L. (1997). Late adulthood suicide: A life-span analysis of suicide notes. *Archives of Suicide Research*, 3, 91–108.

Brevard, A., Lester, D., & Yang, B. (1990). A comparison of suicide notes written by suicide completers and attempters. *Crisis, 11* (1), 7–11.

Canetto, S.S., & Lester, D. (1999). Motives for suicide in suicide notes from women and men. *Psychological Reports, 85*, 471–472.

Leenaars, A.A. (1988). Are women's suicides really different from men? *Women &*

Health, 14, 17--33.

Leenaars, A. (1991). Suicide notes and their implications for intervention. *Crisis, 12* (1), 1–20.

Leenaars, A. (1992). Suicide notes of the older adult. *Suicide and Life-Threatening Behavior, 22* (1), 62–79.

Leenaars, A. A., & Lester, D. (1999). Suicide notes in alcoholism. *Psychological Reports, 85,* 363–364.

Lester, D. (1997). *Making Sense of Suicide: An In-depth Look at Why People Kill Themselves.* Philadelphia: The Charles Press.

Lester, D., & Heim, N. (1992). Sex differences in suicide notes. *Perceptual and Motor Skills, 75,* 582.

Lester, D., & Reeve, C. (1982). The suicide notes of young and old people. *Psychological Reports,* 50, 334.

Shneidman, E. S. (1981). The psychological autopsy. *Suicide and Life-Threatening Behavior,* 11(4), 325–340.

Tuckman J., Kleiner, R. J., & Lavell, M. (1959). Emotional content of suicide notes. *American Journal of Psychiatry*, 116, 59–63.

Evaluation of Postvention Policies and Programs

Loo, R. (1987). Policies and programs for mental health in law enforcement organizations. *Canada's Mental Health*, September, 18–22.

Paton, M. Q. (1980). *Qualitative Evaluation Methods.* Newbury Park, CA: Sage.

Patton, M. Q. (1986). *Utilization-focussed Evaluation.* Newbury Park, CA: Sage. Publications.

Posavac, E. J., & Carey, R. G. (1985). *Program Evaluation: Methods and Case Studies.* Englewood Cliffs, NJ: Prentice Hall.

Rossi, P. H., & Freeman, H. E. (1989). *Evaluation: A systematic approach.* Newbury Park, CA: Sage.

Appendix

ADDITIONAL RESOURCES

Web Sites

Australia
>   Lifeline Melbourne (www.lifeline.org.au)

Canada
>   Canadian Association for Suicide Prevention (www.suicideprevention.ca)
>   Suicide Information & Education Centre (www.siec.ca)

United Kingdom
>   The Samaritans (www.samaritans.org.uk)

USA
>   American Association of Suicidology (www.suicidology.org)
>   American Foundation for Suicide Prevention (www.afsp.org)
>   Suicide Prevention Advocacy Network (www.spanusa.org)
>   Suicide Awareness (www.save.org)

Videos

The company, Films for the Humanities & Sciences (P.O. Box 2053, Princeton, NJ 08543-2053, 1-800-257-5126) offers an extensive variety of focused and affordable videos addressing many of our concerns in postvention. A partial listing of relevant videos is presented; visit their website at www.films.com for a complete listing.

- Suicide and the Police Officer
- Suicide Survivor
- Beyond Stress (a series of six videos)
- Reducing Stress
- Understanding Depression
- Depression: Beyond the Blues

Chapter 9

POLICE SUICIDES: RESPONDING TO THE NEEDS OF THE FAMILY

Teresa T. Tate

The Other Side Of The Wall*

*In Washington, DC
in Judiciary Square
there stands a blue-gray
marble wall with the names
of more than 14,000
men and women.
This is the official list of the
National Law Enforcement
Officers killed in the line of duty.*

*But, there is
ANOTHER SIDE OF THIS WALL
also containing a list
with at least three times
as many numbers
-and steadily growing-
of those men and women
who were victims of
an American war.*

*They died away
from the streets of battle
so they are not as noticeable.*

*Original poem written by John Rowan for the Vietnam Veterans. This version was modified by Cheryl Rehl-Hahn, with permission from the author, to reflect the suicide tragedies taking place daily among our American law enforcement officers.

Their deaths were self inflicted,
ending years of inner torment,
and surmounting stress,
related to tragedies they
witnessed everyday.

But no matter how they died,
they were still Police Officers.
Victims of a war fought
right here on the battlefields
of American streets.
And the list will continue to grow
on the other side of the wall
until those of us still living can
win the war on prevention with
proper education and awareness
of this tragic epidemic.

There are many calls for police assistance in a night, but one of the most disturbing is when a police officer has died by suicide. The actions and reactions of the police chief down to the patrol officer will forever be remembered by a survivor. The trauma that survivors experience may vary from visual effects, to improper notification, to department speculation, and lack of compassion toward survivors. The survivor, as well as the police department, will embark on a painful journey for years to come.

The act of taking one's own life occurs in many different places (i.e., the home, the backyard, the police station, in a squad car, or in a remote area). Ultimately, it is either a family member or a co-worker who discovers the body. Whether the warning signs were visible or occurred by complete surprise, suicide is a death of many unanswered questions.

SUICIDE IN THE HOME

When the suicide occurs in the home, a family member may be present and either witnesses the act or hear the fatal shot. The trauma to the survivor has begun. Most survivors have the instinct to dial 911 for assistance. Once the patrol officers have arrived on the scene, they should escort the survivor from the room where the suicide has occurred. On completion of the initial interview, if the need for any field tests for fingerprints or gun powder residue are required, it should be conducted at this time. These tests should be handled as expeditiously as possible. The survivor may have physical evidence on their face, hands, and clothing. Requiring the survivor to remain in clothing that is covered in blood is increasing the trauma.

If the deceased officer is employed in a jurisdiction other than where he resides, immediate efforts should be made to contact that department's chief of police or field supervisor. The family will be able to provide the name of the supervisor, as well as the telephone number. Notification to the officer's department should be made by telephone as soon as possible. Avoid the use of the Emergency Operations Center (EOC) to connect to the officer's department through the radio. Reporters and the public scan police radios. This will only create a media frenzy at the scene.

In most cases, interviewing the family member at the home in a controlled environment is not only permissible, but suggested. Attempting to escort the survivor from the home while the body is still present is not advisable. Survivors are reluctant to allow separation from the deceased officer until the body is removed from the home. It is also worthy to note that survivors will become increasingly agitated and uncomfortable with the number of police personnel intruding into the home. Limit the number of detectives and forensic technicians in the home so as to not create additional chaos for the family.

Although many survivors are unaware of police procedures, the investigating officer should understand the trauma that was witnessed by the survivor. Survivors who were present when the suicide occurred will not understand the intrusion of personal questions. The survivor will have difficulty in comprehending questions after witnessing the suicide. Although it is the responsibility of the investigating officer to exclude the possibility of a homicide, survivors will become distraught at the thought of being a suspect and not a victim.

When an individual has experienced a traumatic event, the senses may become more alert. Survivors may have the ability to hear several conversations within various parts of the house. While police personnel are investigating the scene, there will be a number of people standing outside the home waiting to perform their duties. Patrol officers, EMS, and coroners should be advised to keep the level of conversation to a minimum. Many people will invoke humor when involved in a stressful situation, but sensitivity toward the family should be the first priority. Survivors will not forget the actions or comments of on-scene personnel for years to come.

Many police departments have established crisis intervention teams to respond to critical incidents. If offering the services of the team to the family, be specific as to how the team was developed, what the team may provide, and identify the experiences of the individuals who comprise the team. Most survivors will not understand the concept of a crisis intervention team unless it is fully explained to them. Although survivors may be reluctant to accept the offer because of the connection to the police department, a team member may be assigned to the family to assist in support, funeral arrangements, or even as a liaison between the family and the department.

If the deceased officer used a firearm to complete suicide, explain to the survivor that the firearm must be surrendered as evidence. If the firearm used was a personally owned firearm and not department issued, the department must take the necessary care in returning the firearm to the family on completion of the investigation. Survivors may have the need to take control of the weapon that caused the death. There are instances in which the firearm was surrendered and destroyed, thrown into a river, and even sold for financial needs. The survivor should be offered the choice as to whether they wish to have the firearm returned.

On completion of the on-scene investigation, the survivor should not be left alone until a family member, other than a member of the household, a friend, or a neighbor is able to arrive at the home. It should be suggested that the survivor, accompanied by the arriving neighbor or friend, leave the home until the opportunity to sanitize the room has been completed. Police departments should have a listing of emergency disaster sanitation companies or janitorial companies available. It is essential that survivors are not left to clean the area. It is also important that survivors are aware that they should contact their homeowners insurance agent for possible reimbursement of repairs or replacement of carpet, walls, bedding, and furniture.

NOTIFICATION

When the death occurs away from the home, there tends to be less trauma inflicted on the survivor. They did not witness the act and generally do not discover the body. There was no physical evidence to be seen. In a study conducted by Survivors of Law Enforcement Suicide (S.O.L.E.S.), 69 percent of police suicides occurred away from the home. The reasons may not be well known, but one could speculate that perhaps the officer was preserving the home for the surviving spouse and children. It may also be ascertained that when the suicide occurs away from the home, the act may have been planned and was not an act of impulse.

When the suicide occurs without the presence or knowledge of the family, the police department should ensure that notification is made directly to the surviving spouse or surviving parent, if the officer was not married. Notification should be made by a supervisor, accompanied by a police chaplain. If a police chaplain is not available, use the services of the department's victim/witness advocate or a crisis counselor.

If making notification at the residence or place of employment of the spouse, police personnel should arrive in an unmarked car. Care should be taken that the death notification is not given until all parties are inside of the house or in a private office. The notifying party should also ascertain the location of the officer's children before breaking the news. For preventive reasons, an ambulance should be parked one or two blocks away from the residence until notice is received that the family members are stable. The shock of hearing the news may bring about a panic or heart attack.

The first response that the family may have is shock and denial. The family may ask questions to which answers are not yet available. Because notification should be made within the first hour of discovering the body, the notifying party will not have specific details of the death. Do not speculate or provide information that has not been confirmed. Let the family know that all their questions will be answered as soon as the information is available.

As a courtesy, ask the spouse if there are additional firearms in the house. If there are young children living in the house, advise the spouse that you are ensuring that the guns are not loaded and are stored in a safe place. Do not attempt to remove the firearms from the home unless requested by the spouse. The removal of personal property without the consent of the spouse will be considered a threatening act.

In cases in which the officer is separated or divorced and the children reside with the former spouse, ensure the same courtesy to the divorced spouse as to the surviving spouse. The ex-spouse will have the difficult task of informing the children of the death.

RETURNING PERSONAL EFFECTS

The funeral home will surrender the officer's jewelry and clothing, if requested, to the family. However, the investigating police department will have possession of items that may have been found with the deceased officer. Such items may include a wallet, keys, money, police badge, a suicide note, and the firearm.

> Several weeks after the funeral, I was allowed to retrieve some of my husband's personal items. I was most anxious to have the house keys returned to me. When I arrived at the police barracks, I was presented with two brown bags. Each bag was sealed with tape and an evidence label. I signed for the two bags and left. Upon arriving home, I opened one bag which contained his keys, a comb and a few dollars. Painful, but not traumatic. The second bag contained the empty shotgun shell that ended his life, empty beer cans and an empty bottle of bourbon that was splattered with blood.

Discretion should be used when returning personal items to the family. The most important item that a survivor would want returned is the suicide note. That note contains the officer's final thoughts, last words, and may provide insight to the question of *why*, which will continue to go unanswered. A simple solution to avoid distressing the survivor is to make a copy of the note before any tests being conducted. Return a copy of the note to the survivor as soon as possible.

> The note that my husband wrote to me was more of a love note than a suicide note. He first asked for forgiveness and then said how he could not go on any longer. He wrote instructions on where he wanted to be laid to rest. He instructed me on how to return the police issued equipment. The note provided me with the knowledge of his last thoughts, always looking out for me.

> I was forced to surrender the note that night as evidence. I read it over and over, committing it to memory. The investigating officer said I would

get it back. And when the note was finally returned to me months later, it had been destroyed. The note had been submerged in a purple liquid for fingerprint testing, so I was told. Those last words had vanished from the paper. I was left with nothing.

The one item that I so desperately needed, was the hardest piece of evidence to retrieve. How ironic that it was easier for me to obtain the shotgun that ended his life than his final words of goodbye.

Large police departments have the opportunity to reassign the deceased officer's patrol car to another precinct to protect the family from seeing the officer's car on patrol. It is unfortunate that with limited budgets, police departments cannot eliminate the car, even if the officer completed suicide inside the vehicle. Not only is it painful for the family to continually see the car on patrol, but it can bring discontent to the officer who is now assigned the vehicle.

FUNERAL PROTOCOL

There has been much debate about whether or not a police officer who dies by suicide should receive the same funeral protocol as an officer who was killed in the line of duty. Should funerals be dictated by how a person died instead of how they lived? Should our final goodbyes be a reflection of shame and disgrace instead of sorrow for not knowing how to help? The first public response the family will receive is that of the police department. Family members should be able to look on the reactions of the police department as compassionate and sensitive. However, not everyone is prepared to handle the suicide of a police officer.

Police departments need to develop a policy on funeral protocol that will allow the officers to express their grief, offer condolences to the family, and participate in memorials. Police administrators do not have the right to dictate how an officer may grieve, for instance, the issue of whether or not an officer should attend the services in uniform or street clothes. This is an individual decision and should be made by each officer. Some officers may wish to offer a final salute in uniform, whereas others, based on their own personal reasons and beliefs, may refuse to wear their uniform. Either option should be acceptable and respected.

The night before the memorial service, the chief of police called and asked if he could wear his uniform to the memorial service. I was a bit confused as to why he would ask such a question and he stated that he was informed that I forbid any officer to wear their uniform.

When I arrived at the chapel for the memorial service, there were no police cars in the parking lot. As I walked down the aisle with the police chaplain, there was not a police uniform in sight. I was distraught to think that none of his peers had come.

It was not I, who refused the wearing of the uniforms, it was his supervisor.

Mistakes can be easily made when assisting the family with the funeral arrangements. Ask the family what services they would like performed at the memorial service and funeral. Determine what services the department is willing to offer. Most police families do not know what a police funeral will entail. If the department is willing to provide an honor guard, a bagpipe player, or a final radio call, explain each service to the family and allow them to choose which options they would like. It is strongly recommended that a firearm salute be omitted from the funeral. When assisting in the funeral arrangements, use care when offering the services that may be performed.

A small police department had experienced their first police suicide. A friend of the deceased officer, who was also a police officer, was assigned as liaison between the family and the department. The department wanted to pay tribute to their officer with a police funeral. The young widow agreed to the funeral arrangement without the full knowledge of the protocol.

At the graveside service, a firearm salute began. Upon hearing the shots fired, the widow became severely distraught and emotional. No one could calm or comfort her. Hearing those shots triggered a response that the department was not prepared to handle. The young widow, who witnessed her husband's death, was only inches away from her husband when he pulled the trigger.

If the family chooses to have a viewing at the funeral home on the day preceding the funeral, it is recommended that the officer's peers arrive at the funeral home 30 minutes before the scheduled wake. Because family members may not personally know the officer's peers, the supervising officer should formally introduce each officer to the spouse or parents. It is also advisable that before meeting the family, the officers have been instructed on how to offer condolences. Simple phrases, such as "I'm sorry for your loss" or "I will miss him or her" will provide comfort to the grieving family. This may be the first time an officer has attended a funeral, and he or she may need assistance in knowing how to express sympathy. As with any funeral arrangements, ask the surviving family if receiving the officer's peers during an arranged time is desired.

If the reactions of the police department have been supportive and compassionate toward the family, the family may wish to express their gratitude publicly. This is usually accomplished during the memorial service. Although the family may be too distraught to speak, either a family representative or a member of the police department may be asked to read a note from the family.

BENEFITS

There are few benefits available to the family of a police officer who completes suicide. However, it would be most appropriate for the department's senior personnel employee to respond to the home, accompanied by the officer's supervisor, to deliver beneficiary forms to the spouse. An appointment should be made with the spouse for a time of convenience, preferably within a week of the death. Because of the complexity of insurance forms, it is not recommended to mail the forms to the spouse or request a police officer or supervisor to drop them off.

Benefits should be discussed with the spouse in a quiet setting. If other family members are present, ask one member to remain with the spouse while benefits are explained. The presence of another family member may help the survivor in understanding the benefits. Generally, most family members have been known to take notes to avoid confusion at a later date.

Personnel employees should be prepared to discuss questions concerning life insurance, health insurance, social security benefits, retirement benefits, death annuities, vacation pay, and a final payroll check. Survivors should be advised on issues of probate, if a will was not written. Police departments have contacts throughout the court system and can provide available resources to the family on probate issues.

EMPLOYEE ASSISTANCE PROGRAM (EAP)

Many police departments have instituted a department EAP office, which may provide outside resources for counseling on personal issues, financial issues, or legal issues. Although most EAP programs are designed for the use by an employee, these programs should be readily accessible to family members as well. Even though there is much speculation among police officers as to the confidentiality of EAP, police departments should ensure that all employees understand the purpose and services that are offered through EAP.

> I was employed by a Federal law enforcement agency at the time of my husband's death. Within two weeks, the EAP office within my agency had provided me with the services of a financial counselor, an attorney and a therapist. The first six sessions with my therapist were free.

> Many years and two Federal agencies later, I had the opportunity to review my official personnel file. Although I assumed that it was recorded in my personnel file that I utilized the services of EAP, there was no evidence to indicate it. All subsequent employers were never aware of my past.

When a police officer dies by suicide, the medical benefits cease. Families struggle to provide for the needs of the children but are left without the most important benefit, health insurance. Without health insurance, spouses and children are unable to receive grief counseling. When the parent of a child completes suicide, what prevents the child from thinking that that act was acceptable? There is evidence that families with the completed suicide of one member are at elevated risk for an additional suicide. Given the tremendous potential impact of suicide on the communication processes of families, and the risk of future suicides, postvention with suicide survivor families should also be considered an important means of prevention of future suicides (Jordan, 2000). Police departments need to implement a benefit for the survivors of a police suicide. By Use of the EAP office, the department can offer families free counseling sessions or offer referrals at a reduced rate. It is unfathomable to think that survivors can learn to cope without the help of a grief therapist. Grief is a powerful emotion, and survivors may begin to believe that they are going crazy or may not be "normal." It is important to remind survivors that they are having normal reactions to an abnormal situation.

At present, there are no national police organizations that offer support to police survivors of suicide. Survivors have had to find support on their own. Police widows have had the unfortunate fate of learning that there is a difference in support, not only financial but emotional, of a survivor of suicide and a survivor of a line of duty death.

> It is my annual crusade to request that survivors of police suicides be included in certain events during Police Week, most importantly, grief seminars. To my dismay, I was told that the liability would be too great since survivors of suicide would jump off the roof of the hotel. In all the Survivors of Suicide Conferences that I have attended, I am happy to report that we all exited the hotel the same way we entered . . . through the door.

There are various outside resources available to survivors. SOLES maintains a national list of survivor of suicide support groups sponsored by the American Foundation for Suicide Prevention (AFSP) and the American Association of Suicidology (AAS) that are available in each state. The American Association of Retired Persons (AARP) sponsors widow/widower support groups nationwide. It is also recommended to survivors that they attend survivor conferences, which provide workshops on grief and suicide issues.

Support groups, conferences, and support of friends and family are beneficial to the family. However, there is a much greater need for grief therapy that cannot be attained from support groups.

INVESTIGATIVE REPORTS

In the months that follow the death, the initial shock of losing their loved one to suicide will begin to subside. Survivors may have questions that were never answered by the investigators and may continue to search for clues as to why the death occurred. When the death occurs away from the home, the survivor may have doubt as to whether the death was an actual suicide. Survivors have been known to reject that the suicide occurred, especially if the survivors were not aware of the warning signs of suicide; a suicide note was not left behind; or if the family was unable to view the body.

There have been instances where the survivors have the need to review the investigative report and photos. Although the department may not understand this need and may have attempted to shield the family from additional trauma, it is imperative to the survivor that they understand how the officer died. Survivors are searching for proof and validation that the suicide occurred. Lingering questions in a survivor's mind will prevent them from obtaining acceptance or even closure. In most instances, it is the surviving spouse who expresses the need to view the photos.

There are steps that the investigating officer should take before arranging for the survivor to view the photos. The officer should take extreme caution to only allow photos with the least amount of trauma to be seen by the survivor. Such photos may include those taken from a distance, at an angle where the entry or exit wound is not viewable; and general nonintrusive photos of the scene. Investigators should be aware that this is not curiosity on the survivors part, but a need to know how and where the officer died.

When the investigator meets with the survivor, it is recommended that the survivor review the photos on a weekend or in the evening when staffing is at a minimum. This will ensure the survivor privacy and allow ample time to review the photos. The presumption that the survivor will become emotional is inevitable.

CONCLUSION

When a loved one dies unexpectedly, the shock is overwhelming. But when the person dies by suicide, the news is devastating. It is important to understand the thought process of a survivor of suicide. In the days, weeks, and months that follow the death, the survivor is in shock and emotionally numb. They may be unable to comprehend and accomplish simple tasks. Survivors may appear to be in control while in public, but many of them have difficulty reappearing in the community. Survivors may feel the need to relocate or change jobs, depending on the events preceding the suicide. Grief is a long-term process and seems to never end.

There are various reasons why a police officer may complete suicide. Reasons may include depression, posttraumatic stress disorder, other mental illnesses, alcohol and substance abuse, alleged misconduct, and infidelity. Although the police department may look to the family for reasons why the suicide occurred, the family may, in turn, look to the department. There are cases in which the family had no clue that the officer was contemplating suicide. But then again, there are cases in which the family knowingly hid the officer's depression in order to protect the officer from possible administrative action.

In instances in which the officer may be under investigation for alleged misconduct, discretion for the family is imperative. Although each person may have their personal opinion as to the character of the officer, public comments should be avoided. Many times, the media will publish quotes from an anonymous source that only inflicts more pain on the survivors. Is it necessary for the department to embarrass the family more than the humiliation that the officer has already established? The events that led up to the officer's suicide ends at the time of death. The surviving family is left with the painful knowledge of those events and will struggle to overcome the shame that has been left behind.

The conduct and attitude of the police department may determine whether additional trauma and anger will be experienced by the survivors. Although anger is a stage in the grief process, it should not be brought about by the insensitive comments and responses of the police department. Survivors will become angry for their loss of a spouse or partner, a parent, and even an adult child. The anger will evolve in time when the survivor must be responsible for daily family activities, such as home and car repairs, payment of bills, celebrating holidays alone, the birthdays of their children, missing the birth of their grandchildren, and even the successes and accomplishments of their own children. The lives of survivors will forever be bittersweet knowing that for every joy they experience, there is also a void.

It is unfortunate that our society is still uneducated about mental illness in the twenty-first century. The issue of blame, shame, and guilt creates the stigma surrounding suicide. Police officers seek medical assistance for broken bones, colds, allergies, physicals, and rashes but hesitate in seeking medical assistance on mental health issues. Should the brain, which is the ultimate organ in the body, be dismissed because of fear of losing one's job or friends? Does society not understand that the brain can become ill like any other organ? Police administrators and police officers need to understand that mental illness is treatable. The time to address the problem is in the beginning and not at the critical point when the officer is in crisis and holding a loaded firearm to his head.

Survivors will, most likely, have feelings of abandonment, rejection, and betrayal, not only by their officer but possibly by the police department as well. The depth of a survivor's pain and despair is multilevel. There are no set time tables for grief. It is important to understand the role of the police department in responding to survivors. Be compassionate and sensitive. Know what community resources are available. Be prepared.

Immediate Response

1. *Police personnel making notification should arrive in unmarked cars.*
2. *Include the police chaplain or crisis counselor when making notification to the family.*
3. *An ambulance should be parked several blocks from the site of notification.*
4. *Ask the survivor who should be contacted for emotional support (i.e., a family member, neighbor, or a friend).*
5. *Do not speculate or provide information that has not been confirmed.*
6. *Advise the family what will be said at the press conference, if one will be given.*
7. *Notify all police personnel that speaking to the media, even on condition of anonymity, is prohibited.*
8. *Assign a police officer or police chaplain to act as the liaison between the department and the family.*

Within 48 Hours

1. *The liaison officer has notified the department of the funeral arrangements.*
2. *Notification of funeral arrangement is provided to other jurisdictions, as well as city council, mayor's office, etc.*
3. *Arrangements should be made with other police jurisdictions to pro-*

vide patrol support so that police officers, dispatchers, and other personnel may attend the funeral.

4. *A benefits package (i.e., life insurance, health insurance, annuities), should be presented to the family by a qualified personnel employee.*
5. *Copy and return a copy of the suicide note.*

REFERENCE

Jordan, J.R. (2000). Is Suicide Bereavement Different? *The Forum Newsletter* (p.3).

Chapter 10

POLICE SUICIDE PREVENTION: CONCLUSIONS AND FUTURE DIRECTIONS

JOHN M. VIOLANTI

We are presently faced with many challenges in police suicide prevention efforts. Those challenges remain steadfast in the path of successful prevention. We have not yet learned the prevalence and incidence of suicide in law enforcement. We only know that, in most cases, the rate is higher than other working or general populations. The obvious solution is to conduct further and more careful research on a wider scale. Working on denial by police departments that suicide is a problem is no easy task. It seems, however, through the efforts of groups like The Law Enforcement Wellness Association (LEWA) and Survivors of Law Enforcement Suicide (SOLES) that police agencies are beginning to understand the seriousness of suicide risk in police work. There is also a lack of sufficient information as to why police suicide occurs, calling for more in-depth research into the lives and experiences of those officers who do commit suicide.

Hackett's discussion in Chapter 2 about the supervisory role in suicide prevention is important. Police supervisors are important persons in the lives of street officers, and they are more willing to take advice for help from a supervisor than from other sources. The role of police peer support as a "safe place" for officers to seek help also makes considerable sense in prevention. If police officers are unwilling to seek help from formal mental health sources, certainly other peer officers trained in basic intervention are good alternatives. Clark and White, in the discussion of clinicians and the police, reiterate this point. They emphasize that impact on the police career, shame, and mistrust of mental health professions are primary reasons why police are afraid to seek help for distress. The police believe that they are problem solvers, not people with problems, so they opt out of getting help. Clark and White's ideas about involving all support mechanisms such as the family, friends, and peers are important to prevention efforts.

Quinnet and Watson's "QPR" (question-persuade-refer) method discussed in Chapter 4 provides laypersons, police peer counselors, and mental health professionals an excellent additional tool for preventing suicide within the ranks. QPR is a simple and straightforward method of prevention. It is often co-workers on the force who may be in the best position to see warning signs of risk that could lead to a life-saving intervention. Similarly, spouses and family members may pick up on different clues. More opportunities for early intervention exist when members of a socially integrated organization (including families) are trained to recognize a potential suicide crisis in progress and are trained in what steps to take to interrupt the suicidal journey.

Diamond's discussion of depression as a major factor in police suicide points to a different perspective. Previous ideas have focused on individual aspects that may lead to police suicide, such as posttraumatic stress disorder (PTSD), stress, relationships. Dr. Diamond comments that these factors may indeed be precipitants for police suicide, but that we must recognize that they first result in depression. He advises police managers and departments to have familiarity with depression, because it affects such a high percentage of officers, especially when this depression is associated with a significant risk for suicide. Officers who have worked in particularly stressful environments, or who have encountered significant traumatic situations on the job, will experience an even greater impact.

The police culture and its impact on suicide is discussed by Violanti in Chapter 6. The process of resocialization from civilian to police officer is very strong in training and continues to dominate officers' lives throughout their career. The perspective of solving life problems through the "cognitive lenses" of the police culture can constrict and limit an officer's ability to cope with stress. It may also prevent officers from seeking help for their problems, because they fear shame within the realm of their peers. The police culture may thus have a negative impact on the mental health and life circumstances of police officers, which may increase the potential for suicide.

Dr. Greene's ideas concerning trust as an important factor in officers seeking help is interesting. The more that peers and others seek to help the troubled officer, the more mistrusting the officer becomes. This sort of behavior may also be linked to the influence of the police culture and the underlying ethos of the police working personality to be constantly "suspicious." If the officer comes to mistrust his or her peers and friends, certainly he or she will not trust a mental health professional.

What happens in a department after a suicide can be devastating. Quite often, entire departments succumb to a depressed mood, and productivity falls. There is often a grief wave in the department when an officer suicides. Police administrators have commented that somehow their officers do not seem the same after a suicide; supervisors notice an effect on morale, happiness, and work. This emphasizes the need to recognize and prevent suicides among police personnel. Loo's "postvention" involves a designed plan to help reduce the negative impact on departments and family. Postvention is essential, because it allows for the proper grieving of survivors and departments. Postvention shows that someone cares enough to be concerned about those who survive suicide. Police leaders should arrange for psychological debriefings after the suicide of an officer that will help individual survivors and the department deal with the crisis.

One of the most distressing events in law enforcement is the suicide of an officer. For survivors, the sudden or unexpected death of a loved one can be a traumatic life event. Although most duty-related deaths are distressful, suicide may create even more trauma for survivors. It is unfortunate that survivors of police suicide must not only deal with their own grief but also with negative reactions of police peers, the organization, and the public. The police work group has the *potential* to provide a supportive set of conditions in reducing psychological distress, because it provides environmental structure, leadership, companionship and a source of motivation for recovery. Quite often, however, survivors of police suicide are abandoned more quickly than those of officers who died from other causes. Police officials may not place much emphasis on assisting survivors of police suicide because of the stigma associated with such deaths. Theresa Tate, founder of Survivors of Law Enforcement Suicide (SOLES), discussed in her chapter about how the police agency can better help survivors of suicide. The actions and reactions of the police chief down to the patrol officer will forever be remembered by a survivor. The trauma that survivors experience may vary from visual effects, to improper notification, to department speculation, and lack of compassion toward survivors. The survivor, as well as the police department, may embark on a painful journey for years to come.

FUTURE RESEARCH CONSIDERATIONS

Psychological autopsies may be an important research tool in determining police suicide precedents. The issues of stress, PTSD, alcohol use, depression, and relationship problems must be further explored. This research design will allow us to examine risk factors reportedly associated with police suicide. Most previous studies on police suicide provide evidence of high risk, but fall short in explaining precipitant individual and social factors involved in police suicide. This lack of information impedes efforts at suicide prevention among the police, other similar occupations, and specific age groups. In future work, we must use a better, more valid design. The "psychological autopsy" is well established as the means for obtaining comprehensive retrospective information about victims of completed suicide.

PSYCHOLOGICAL AUTOPSY HYPOTHESES

The following are ideas about why police officers might decide to choose suicide:

- Police officers who commit suicide will more often have suffered from current active and lifetime diagnoses of major affective disorders, substance abuse disorders, and their comorbidity.
- Police suicide victims are more likely to have experienced severe violence at work in their lifetime.
- Police officers who commit suicide will (1) have experienced

more life event stressors; and (2) have smaller social networks, with which they interact less frequently, and which they derive less instrumental support.

- Police officers who have a history of alcohol abuse are more likely to complete suicide.
- Police officers have instant access to firearms, which they use in work. We hypothesize that police officers will be more likely to complete suicide with a firearm than other methods.
- Police officers are hesitant and untrusting when it comes to visiting health care professionals. No study has yet investigated whether police officers who go on to commit suicide are more or less likely to have asked for help from an Employee Assistance Program or mental health professional.
- Police officers who commit suicide will be more likely to have been exposed to or involved in stressful traumatic events in their work.

CONCLUSION

The issues highlighted in this book deserve serious consideration to advance police suicide prevention. A number of medical, psychological, and social influences seem to be associated with police suicide, and knowledge of these influences is necessary to reach that goal.

All too often we emphasize the dangers of police work but seem to neglect the hidden psychological danger of this profession. Suicide is a consequence of that hidden danger. It is a clear indication of the intolerable strain placed on the police officer's work and life roles. At the least, we should adequately address this problem and provide methods and means to prevent future tragedies.

AUTHOR INDEX

A

(AAS) American Association of
　　Suicidology, 55, 65
Allen, S.W., 31, 36
Alpert, G.P., 75
Anjeski, 43, 52
(APA) American Psychiatric
　　Association, 88, 101

B

Baker, L., 14
Baker, J. , 41, 52
Baker, T., 12, 14, 41, 52
Bauer, M.N., 97, 102
Bailey, W.G., 75
Berman, A.L., 97,102
Beskow, J., 102
Bibb, J.L., 97, 102
Blau, T.H., 74
Blumenthal, S.J., 73, 75
Bonafacio, P., 69, 71, 74
Brent, D.A., 94, 102
Brevard, A., 96, 102
Brown, M.K., 71, 74

C

Cain, A.C., 102, 103
Calhoun, L., 93, 102
Campbell, T., 71 74
Canetto, S., 97, 102
Clark, D.W., 3, 4, 14, 16, 36
Clawson, M., 41, 52
Conroy, R.W., 70, 74

D

Dash, J., 74,
Diamond, D., 3, 54, 121
Dixon, J.F., 97, 102
Dunham, R.G., 75
Durkheim, E., 71, 72, 74
Dyregrov, A., 92, 101

F

Farberow, N.L., 91, 101,102
Field, G., 7, 15, 40, 52
Freeman, H.E., 103
Freud, S., 74

G

Gilmartin, K.M., 67, 74
Goldstein, H.A., 75
Greene, C.L., 5, 76, 121
Gross, E., 68, 74
Guralnick, L., 66, 74

H

Hackett, D.P., xxi, 3, 7
Hargrave, G., 73, 74
Harris, R.N., 67, 68, 74
Heim, N., 97
Hill, K.O., 41, 52
Honig, A.L., 6, 21
Hyatt, D., 73, 74

I

Ivanoff, A., 66, 70, 74

SUBJECT INDEX

A

Adaptations, psychological, 20
    Alcohol, use of, 21
    "Choir practice," 21
    Coping , 21
    Shutting off, 20
AFSP (American Foundation for Suicide
    Prevention), 51
Alcoholism, 96
All-or-nothing thinking, police, 69
Antidepressant drugs, 58
Awareness training, suicide, 74

B

"Bad fit," 8
Barriers to treatment, police agency, 54
Benefits, police, 113
Brotherhood of biochemistry, 67

C

Case-by-case approach, 62
Chicago PD, 7
CISD, 89
Clues, suicide, 45-46
    Coded, 45
    Behavioral, 45
    Direct, 45
    Situational, 45
Cognitive constriction, suicide and, 69–70
    "All-or-nothing thinking," police, 69
    Lack of flexible thinking, 73
Communications, suicide, 45–47, 51
    Coded clues, 45

Dire predictions, 46
    Red light, 46
Confidentiality issues, police, 17
    Chambers review, 18
    Job impact worries, 18
    Job loss, 19
    Medical records, 18
    Medications, use of, 21
    Mental stability, 19
    Mistrust of Mental Health professionals,
      21
    Stigma, emotional problems, 20
Cops on the edge, 17
Crisis intervention teams, survivors, 108
Culture, police, 3, 66-68
    Cohesiveness of, 68
    Impact of, 68
    Formal, informal, 68

D

Depersonaliztion, 70
Depression, clinical, 3, 55, 58-61
Distancing, suicide signs, police, 76
"Dry run," 79

E

EAP assistance, 113-114

F

FBI, 7, 40
Firearm, police use of, suicide, 109–110
Funeral protocol, 24, 111–113
    Departmental policy, 111